Eric P Roth

Gen. 12:3

They Thought
for
Themselves

They Thought for Themselves

for

Themselves

DARING TO CONFRONT THE FORBIDDEN

SID ROTH

DESTINY IMAGE® PUBLISHERS, INC.

P.O. Box 310, Shippensburg, PA 17257-0310

"Speaking to the Purposes of God for This Generation and for the Generations to Come."

This book and all other Destiny Image, Revival Press, MercyPlace, Fresh Bread, Destiny Image Fiction, and Treasure House books are available at Christian bookstores and distributors worldwide.

For a U.S. bookstore nearest you, call 1-800-722-6774.

For more information on foreign distributors, call 717-532-3040.

Or reach us on the Internet: www.destinyimage.com.

Previous ISBN 0-910267-02-2

Previously copyrighted © 1996 by Sid Roth; Reprinted 1999, 2002, 2005.

Paperback:	Hardcover:
ISBN 10: 0-7684-2842-4	ISBN 10: 0-7684-3135-2
ISBN 13: 978-0-7684-2842-1	ISBN 13: 978-0-7684-3135-3

For Worldwide Distribution, Printed in the U.S.A.

1 2 3 4 5 6 7 8 9 10 11 / 13 12 11 10 09

Dedication

To Joy

Contents

Introduction

My father was born in Poland into a traditional Jewish family. My mother's family, while also very Jewish, was much more Americanized. Dad won out in our religious education. I attended a traditional synagogue and was trained for bar mitzvah.

Even as a child, I saw the hypocrisy in our religious observance. For instance, on major holidays, we parked several blocks away from the shul because we didn't want the rabbi to know we drove on the Shabbat. And we had to get there early or the other members would take all the best parking spaces.

The long services in Hebrew, a language I didn't understand, added to my boredom and resentment. Why did we go to synagogue? Why all the ritual? Why was God not speaking to us today? Was the Bible from God? These are just a few of the questions that plagued me.

I was proud of being a Jew, but the religious side turned me off. It just wasn't relevant.

For almost 30 years, God was irrelevant to me—until I thought for myself.

This book is the result of a dream I had in which I was instructed to find and interview Jewish people who broke through the mold of their previous experiences to achieve their destiny. Everyone has a special destiny, but few reach it.

The people in this book come from widely divergent backgrounds including a holocaust survivor, a multi-millionaire, a media executive, and a Ph.D. They range in upbringing from atheistic to Orthodox.

What is the common denominator among those in this unusual group?

They all thought for themselves…and dared to confront the forbidden.

If you have ever thought that there must be something more to life, you were right!

CHAPTER 1
BY DAVID YANIV

CHAPTER 1

Paralyzed… "Learn to Live With It!"

I was born in Tel Aviv in 1936 to parents who immigrated from Germany. My parents kept up tradition, celebrating Yom Kippur, Rosh Hashanah, and other holidays, but they were never really religious. After the Second World War, when my father found out that two of his sisters and one brother and their families had been killed in Nazi Germany, he took every Bible and everything in our home that was even remotely religious and threw it out. "Where was God?" he would ask. "How could God allow such a thing to happen?" From then on, I was raised in an atheistic home. My father even resisted my having a bar mitzvah. Although he finally allowed it, he refused to set foot in the synagogue.

> **"How could god allow
> such a thing to happen?"**

In 1960 I married a South African girl named Sheila, whom I met when she and her mother came to Israel as tourists. At the time, I was a guide and a bus driver. Her mother, who took two tours with me, one day said, "My baby is waiting for me in Haifa. I want you to meet her." I thought it was funny that this elderly woman would have a baby. But when I reached Haifa and saw her "baby," I realized she was a matchmaker. Sheila and I went to South Africa on our honeymoon to visit her family—and stayed twelve and one-half years.

I'm a refrigeration and air-conditioning engineer by trade. I did quite well in business in South Africa for a time. Then I undertook a project to air condition a large building. The quantity surveyor I hired to estimate the cost of the job made a mistake, and I lost all my money.

My lawyer told me it was useless to sue the surveyor because he wasn't insured. And even though I was bankrupt, I had to finish the job because I had signed a contract.

The Mistake Paralyzed Me for Life

Afterward, I decided to return to Israel. Moving back was very difficult for my wife, but she realized it was best for us and our two sons, who were 11 and 8 years old. At the time, I spoke Hebrew, but my family did not. We decided to live on a *moshav*, which is an agricultural commune similar to a *kibbutz*.

I thought we would stay there for a short time to allow my family to learn Hebrew, and then I would find work in my trade. But when the time came, and I said, "All right, let's move to the big town," they didn't want to go. They had come to love life on the moshav. Even if they had agreed, however, it would have been difficult to leave. You can't build up any savings there because you only receive a small monthly allowance to buy food and supplies. But if we stayed at the moshav, we were set for life.

The first year on the moshav we had to work in different jobs to allow everyone to get to know us and for us to get to know them. Toward the end of that year I was assigned to milk the cows. I enjoyed it because it was something new and because I knew it was just a temporary assignment.

> **The first year on the moshav we had to work in different jobs to allow everyone to get to know us and for us to get to know them.**

One day in the cow shed I slipped on a wet spot on the floor and fell flat on my back. My back was in so much pain I went to the hospital to have it checked. The hospital technicians didn't find anything serious on the x-rays. They said, "You just got a good knock there. Go home, rest, take some painkillers, and it will be all right within two weeks."

Instead of getting better, the pain got worse. The second time I went to the hospital, they x-rayed me again, and again sent me home saying there was nothing wrong. I rested for another two weeks, and by that time the pain was excruciating. I had never experienced such pain. The painkillers helped initially, but after a while they lost their effect. I kept increasing the dosage until I was taking 50 pills a day for three years.

I reached a point where every morning when I got out of bed my feet would go numb. I knew something was seriously wrong, but I also knew I couldn't go back to that same hospital again.

Because of the bureaucracy in Israel it took some connections to be allowed to go to another hospital, but through friends who knew somebody who knew somebody, it was arranged for me to visit another hospital in Tel Aviv. The doctors there did a special x-ray called a myelogram.

After the x-ray, the head of the neurosurgical department himself came to me and said, "You've got two slipped discs, one of which is completely compressed and the other one is missing a piece." He was amazed I had waited so long to get help.

When I asked for his prognosis, he replied, "Well, we'll have to operate."

"What does that entail?" I asked, cautiously.

"Oh, it's nothing," he said. "Ten days and you're back home as good as new."

That sounded wonderful to me, so I said, "Let's do it."

When I woke up from the anesthetic in the evening after the operation, I had no feeling from my waist down, so I called for a doctor. The doctor on the evening shift said, "I can't tell you anything. You will have to wait until the morning when all the surgeons come in for the day shift."

> **When I woke up from the anesthetic in the evening after the operation, I had no feeling from my waist down.**

The next morning the doctor who had operated came to me and said, "David, I'm terribly sorry. I've got some bad news for you."

Bracing myself, I asked, "What do you mean you've got bad news for me?"

He said, "I made a mistake, and you will be paralyzed for life."

Apparently, he had cut too deeply with his scalpel and severed the nerves that were essential for me to walk. I had no feeling in one leg and only partial feeling in the other.

At first I was in shock. Then I began to feel sorry for myself. I thought, *What am I going to do now? I had pain before, but at least I could walk. If I could only take time back now, I would rather live with the pain.* But I couldn't go back.

A Broken Man

The doctor's prognosis for the future was summed up in one cold sentence: "Learn to live with it." It was very difficult. I hated everybody. I blamed everybody. But worst of all, I absolutely hated myself. I could not accept what had happened.

From the hospital I was sent to a convalescent home called Beth-Levinshtein, which helps paralyzed people, mainly soldiers who get wounded in the war. They also take some private cases, such as mine. There I started to feel a little better about myself because everyone around me was either worse off than I was or in the same condition. The staff made iron calipers (braces) for me which were attached to special shoes. With the help of crutches and the calipers, I could make my way around without a wheelchair, although it was very difficult.

> **But worst of all, I absolutely hated myself. I could not accept what had happened.**

Three and one-half months later, I returned to the moshav to find my home rearranged. My friends had made a ramp so I could easily get into the house with my wheelchair. They installed handles in the bathroom and other places around the house where I would need them. I was very grateful.

But now that I was surrounded by healthy, active people, I began to realize how much of an invalid I was. I started feeling sorry for myself again, so much so that I needed psychiatric treatment. Never in a million years would I have ever thought I would need a psychiatrist. I had always been such a strong person. Suddenly, I was a broken man.

> **Suddenly, I was
> a broken man.**

Before long, the psychiatrist gave up on me because I wouldn't stop feeling sorry for myself. I was the most unhappy person imaginable. I couldn't forgive the doctor. I couldn't forgive anyone.

My condition was also very difficult for my wife, to the point that I was afraid she might leave me. She never did. In fact, she would try to reassure me, telling me not to worry, that she would stay with me through thick and thin. But the more she told me not to worry, the more I worried.

The moshav gave me an easy job in the office where my coworkers were especially kind. But the nicer they were, the worse I felt. I was sure they were giving me special treatment because of my disabilities.

In the midst of my pity parties, I still had hope that I would some day walk again. I read in the newspaper one day about a man who would put his hand on sick people, sending something that felt like an electric current through their bodies, and they would feel better. The moshav offered to pay my expenses, so I went to him. Nothing happened.

Then I heard about a guru. I went to him with the same result. I believed in each one I went to. When you're as desperate as I was, you try anything. The moshav even paid for transcendental meditation. Nothing worked.

Nothing happened.
Nothing worked.

After seven and one-half years of trying everything the world had to offer, I finally gave up. I finally accepted the expert advice of all the specialists, professors, and neuro-surgeons who told me: "Learn to live with it. You are going to remain paralyzed for the rest of your life. Don't even think of getting better." My wife had long since given up hope that my condition would ever improve. She would say, "What are you running after? Accept it. This is how you are going to remain. I've accepted it. Why can't you?"

And, at that point, I really did accept it. I still felt sorry for myself, but I accepted it. I realized that nobody could help me. I determined to go on and try to live as normal a life as I possibly could.

Why Don't You Pray With Me?

One day, I stayed home from work with the flu and was totally bored. At two o'clock that afternoon I decided to watch television. Since Israeli stations only broadcast in the evening, I started watching a program on Lebanese television called *The 700 Club*. I was intrigued by the name, thinking it was an entertainment program.

I soon realized that it was a Christian show. But there was nothing else to do, and I was curious, so I kept watching. Still, I felt like I was doing something wrong, so I locked the door. I didn't want my wife and my children to catch me watching Christian television.

The program held my interest because it featured stories about people who were healed from different sicknesses. The first time I watched, there was an interview with a woman who had been healed of cancer. She showed an x-ray of a tumor the size of an orange. Then she showed an x-ray of the same spot taken three days later. The tumor had disappeared.

I was sure it was phony. These people had to be paid actors. Some of the stories even made me laugh out loud at the absurdity of the claims. Yet, I found myself watching every day at two o'clock—behind locked doors.

After a month of this, I decided to tell my wife. I said, "Sheila, I've been watching this Christian program about people who get healed by believing in Jesus and by people praying for them."

I expected her to be annoyed with me. On the contrary, she said, "If it makes you feel better, keep watching." She even suggested I record it so we could watch it together in the evening.

During every program there was a time when co-host Ben Kinchlow would say, "Pray with me." Whenever it came to that part, I switched off the television. I didn't even want to hear people pray to Jesus. I felt it was wrong.

> **Whenever it came to that part, I switched off the television. I didn't even want to hear people pray to Jesus. I felt it was wrong.**

As I was watching alone one afternoon several months later, it seemed that Ben's finger stretched out from the television pointing straight at me. He said, "You! Why don't you pray with me?" I could have sworn he was talking directly to me. I got scared. The next thing I knew, I found myself praying the sinner's prayer with him. Here I was praying with him to this "Jesus," who to me had never been more than a dirty name. When that prayer was finished, I couldn't believe what I had done. I thought to myself, *What on earth do I do now?*

I immediately told Sheila. Again, she responded more positively than I expected. She said, "If it makes you feel good, you just carry on. But do me a favor. Don't tell anyone about it. Let it be between us for now."

I was sure that I was the only Jewish person in the whole world who had ever prayed that prayer. I thought, *The first thing I have to do is buy a full Bible.* So I went to Nazareth and bought a Bible. At the book store, I saw a map of the city on display, and, somehow, the name of a Baptist church caught my eye.

As I started reading my Bible, I soon discovered there was more to it than I had ever imagined. I found that the prophecies from the Old Testament are fulfilled in the New

Testament. And I started to wonder why Jewish people throughout the centuries had not believed in Jesus.

You Will Be Healed

The following Sunday, I went to the Baptist church at eight o'clock in the morning. I was too early—the doors were locked.

All around me I heard the bells of churches ringing, and here this church was locked! I was just about to leave when an Arab man walked up and introduced himself as the pastor. He first spoke to me in Arabic and then English, because he didn't speak Hebrew. When I told him my story, he was amazed. He said, "We've tried to get Jewish people to come to the Lord for years, and here you're walking in yourself. This is the first time since I've been a pastor that this has happened."

The pastor invited me to stay for the service. Being Jewish in an Arab congregation, I thought I would feel out of place, but I didn't. The love I experienced that day was the love of Jesus.

> **The love I experienced that day was the love of Jesus.**

At the end of the service there was an invitation to come forward to receive the Lord as personal savior. After I came forward, I found myself praying the same prayer I had been praying daily for four and one-half months in

❖ 23 ❖

front of my television. But this time I did it in front of a whole congregation of witnesses.

This was almost too much for my wife. It was one thing to watch a Christian program or pray a prayer in private. It was quite another to make a public profession of faith in Jesus. She was incensed that I would do such a thing without first consulting her.

However, as the weeks went by and she saw that I was steadfast in my decision, she agreed to come with me to a meeting of Jewish believers. Soon afterward, she accepted Jesus too.

About five months after I became a believer in the Messiah, I was again watching *The 700 Club* when co-host Danuta Soderman had a word of knowledge. She said, "There is someone," she didn't specifically say where, "who has been paralyzed halfway down his body for years," and with me that was the case, seven and one-half years. She said, "He will feel a warm sensation running through his body, and he will be healed."

I said, "Oh, please, God, let it be me." I believed it was me, but nothing happened. Still I kept praying because I realized immediately if it wasn't for me, it must have been for someone else.

...all of a sudden a feeling like an electric current ran from my spine down to my tiptoes, and my feet started jumping 40 inches at a time.

That same evening around ten o'clock I was lying in bed reading my Bible, when all of a sudden a feeling like an electric current ran from my spine down to my tiptoes, and my feet started jumping 40 inches at a time.

When people are paralyzed, they get unwanted reflex movements, and I thought that was what this was. Some of them were more severe than others, but I couldn't explain the electric shock. Finally, the movements stopped, and I went to sleep.

The next morning when I woke up, I started to assist my legs with my hands as I usually did in order to get them out of bed. As I touched my legs, all of a sudden I realized I had feeling in them! I thought, *Wait a minute. This is unusual!* I started to touch all the places where I had lost feeling years before. There was feeling in them!

I shouted, "Sheila, for God's sake, come here! I can feel!"

"Rubbish," she said. "Lie down." She took a needle and started pricking me. "Close your eyes. Where am I pricking you?" And she continued pricking me in different places on my legs. Each time she pricked my legs, I told her the correct spot. Now she began to share my excitement.

Immediately, I went to the dispensary on our moshav to see the doctor. I put the special shoes back on because I still didn't know exactly what had happened to me, and, after seven and one-half years of paralysis, my legs had no muscles in them. When our moshav doctor was shocked too, I realized a true miracle had occurred.

> **When our moshav doctor
> was shocked too, I realized a
> true miracle had occurred.**

The moshav doctor sent me to a hospital for an electric test of my reflexes. I had had this test done many times before, and, of course, it was always negative. This time my reflexes responded to the test perfectly. The doctor who performed the test asked if I could return the following week.

A week later, I met with about 25 doctors, neurosurgeons, and neurologists from all over the country, including the neurosurgeon who had operated on me. They all examined me, but no one could give a logical explanation for what had happened. They said it was not possible. Some of them even thought I was lying by claiming that the older x-rays were mine. Even today, doctors who examine them cannot believe that I am walking.

At the end of the examination they said to me, "This is a medical miracle."

I said, "Listen. This is not a medical miracle. This is *Yeshua* (Jesus)."

Someone asked, "Yeshua who?" Yeshua is a very common name in Israel, so he thought perhaps Yeshua was my physiotherapist, or a friend.

> **I said, "Listen. This is**
> **not a medical miracle.**
> **This is _Yeshua_ (Jesus)."**

"Yeshua the Messiah," I responded.

That was too much for these Jewish doctors. They did not want to hear another word about this "Jesus."

They refused to believe He could have had anything to do with my healing. We know from the Bible that even when people saw Jesus perform miracles right before their eyes, they didn't believe. Some even accused Him of being demon possessed.

The doctor said to take off the iron calipers, but to keep using the crutches because my legs were just skin and bones. And slowly, slowly, I took my first steps in seven and one-half years. I knelt down on knees that hadn't felt anything since the accident and thanked the Lord for the miracle He had done.

But He wasn't finished yet. The doctors had told me that the muscles in my legs were all dead and that they would never grow back. Over time, God recreated those muscles. Today, my feet are just as normal as anyone else's.

You Have to Leave

When the members of the moshav saw me walking, they didn't accept that this was the work of Yeshua any more than the doctors did. Instead, they chose to believe the doctors' conclusion that it was a "medical miracle."

It was not long before word had spread around the moshav that I was a believer in Yeshua. The leaders of the moshav called me into their office and said, "We're terribly sorry, but you have to leave. We do not accept Christians on the moshav." This moshav is associated with B'nai B'rith in New York, and they were worried they would lose their funding if they didn't expel me.

I said, "I call myself a 'Messianic Jew,' and I will not go quietly. There is a great big Christian world out there just waiting to hear my story."

Sensing that the publicity generated by expelling me might be worse than if they let me stay, they said I could remain—*if* I promised I would not evangelize on the moshav.

> I said, "I call myself a 'Messianic Jew,' and I will not go quietly. There is a great big Christian world out there just waiting to hear my story."

That arrangement worked fine until May 1988 when I participated in a major Messianic Jewish event in Jerusalem called "Shavuot '88"—at that time the largest gathering of Jewish believers in Israel in almost two thousand years. It seemed that every Hebrew-speaking newspaper in Jerusalem covered the miracle of my healing.

When I came home from the meetings, the moshav leaders said, "That's it. You promised us you would not evangelize. Now your picture is splashed all over the newspapers. B'nai B'rith is going to stop the money flowing to us. You have to leave."

They voted us out at a general meeting and gave us ten days in which to leave. Nobody from the moshav, where we had lived for 16 years, even came to help us pack our belongings.

If God had not made a way, we would have been out in the street and penniless. But we serve a living God! At the gathering somebody had handed me an envelope. As I ripped it open, I couldn't believe my eyes! It contained a scholarship and airline tickets to attend Bible school in Dallas, Texas.

My wife and I graduated in May 1989 and followed the Lord's leading to Seattle, where we live today. I have been healed for well over a decade, and my faith grows deeper every day. Soon we will return to Israel and proclaim the good news about the true Messiah who saves and heals!

Commentary by Sid Roth

I read in the Torah that God heals people. But in 30 years of going to a traditional synagogue I never saw anyone get healed. On television I saw "faith healers" and thought they were all counterfeit. But you can't have a good counterfeit unless there is the real thing. The Talmud, as well as the New

Testament, records healings that occurred when Jewish believers in Jesus prayed to God. The Talmud also warns traditional Jews not to let Messianic Jews (Jewish believers in Jesus) pray for them (Tosefta Chullin, Chapter 2:22-23). This is a backhanded compliment! These rabbis recognized that the Jewish followers of Jesus had power to heal in His Name. And once you experience healing in His Name, you might believe in Him. Isaiah 53:4-5 tells us the Messiah would bear away all our diseases.

But only our diseases did He bear Himself, and our pains carried: while we indeed esteemed Him stricken, smitten of God, and afflicted. Yet He was wounded for our transgressions, He was bruised for our iniquities: the chastisement for our peace was upon Him; and through His bruises was healing granted to us.

The early Messianic Jews, even brand-new believers, experienced miracles of healing in His Name. And since He doesn't change, I too have seen many Jewish people healed in Jesus' Name. My own mother, before becoming a Messianic Jew, was healed in His Name.

CHAPTER 2
BY BARRY MINKOW

CHAPTER 2

ZZZZ Best

I was 21 years old and had it all—or so it seemed. Outwardly, I had achieved the kind of success most people only dream about. ZZZZ Best, the carpet-cleaning company I had started when I was only 16, was now worth $280 million. I had a 5,000 square-foot house in an exclusive community. I drove a Ferrari. I lived with a beautiful woman and dated others on the side. I had made it!

Yet, as I arrived at my 21st birthday party, I was plagued with doubts and insecurities. Every time I had a birthday I was afraid that the "boy wonder" would soon become old news—no longer recognizable—like the athlete who suddenly finds himself overshadowed by some younger, rising star. At age 21 I felt I was getting old.

Worst of all, I was a fraud—a fact I kept well hidden from my friends. They didn't know my company was built on lies and deception.

At age 21 I felt
I was getting old.

With mixed emotions, I descended the stairs of my house to find throngs of people who had come to congratulate me. They all loved me. Or did they? I walked into one room and saw the accountants and lawyers who represented ZZZZ Best, and I thought to myself, *They are here because they keep the books for my company. I wonder if they really like me.* I went to the next room where there was a group of investors, and I thought, *Do they really like me, or are they here because they are making a nice return on their dollar right now?* Then I went outside and greeted a few of the Mafia people with whom I was involved. I knew why they were there— they were making money.

As I walked back into the house I was completely depressed. I didn't know who really cared about me for who I was and not for what I could give them. I walked into the kitchen and saw my best friend and my girlfriend. My girlfriend was wearing a huge diamond ring I had bought her. I had just given my best friend $10,000.

I had bought my way to the top, bought all my allegiances. I didn't know if I had a friend in the world. It was the loneliest moment of my life. I had experienced what I thought would deliver the ultimate satisfaction—money, power, and fame—only to discover that my life was completely bankrupt.

Early Compromise

My life of deception began at the tender age of nine. I was very goal oriented even at that young age. I wanted to be the best at selling newspaper subscriptions. And I was. How did I do it? By telling the customer whatever he wanted to hear just to get the sale. The customer might say, "I just canceled my subscription because I would find my paper out by the curb or under my car all the time." And in order to win the sale, I would promise doorstep delivery with a money-back guarantee. This was something we were told *not* to promise, but I wanted to be the best. I had a desire for recognition.

When people said I was the best, a hero even in this small context, it was a drug in my veins. Once I tasted the recognition, I was hooked. I would do whatever was necessary to achieve that same feeling again and again.

Late one afternoon, I was two sales behind another boy who was working the other side of the street. With only one block to go, I was determined to beat him. Quickly, I sold two subscriptions. But, before long, I found myself at the last house. When I realized no one was home, I got desperate. There was no way I was going to lose. In a burst of inspiration, I made up a name and phone number and signed a phony subscription order, putting me over the top. The rush of being the best again dispelled any fear I had of getting caught.

> **The rush of being the best again dispelled any fear I had of getting caught.**

But I *was* caught. The manager called me and was very nice about the whole thing. He said, "Listen, I know what you did here, and it's OK. I still want you to work for me because I think that you're a great salesman. But I really can't afford to have you make up leads." Every time we got a lead, the newspaper gave us a dollar. He said, "I'll tell you what. I'll give you the dollar if you need the money that bad." He didn't want to lose me because even with all the problems, my sales were still good enough to justify my staying. He said, "Just come clean with me."

I denied it. I said, "I quit. I don't want to hear it." At a very young age I was in denial. Even though I knew I was guilty, I just denied the charge because of the embarrassment it might cause me and my family. After I hung up the phone, I said, "Mom, I'm not going to work there anymore. I think I need to concentrate more on school." There were no other repercussions from my action because the manager dropped the matter. He never called my parents. The absence of any consequences reinforced the behavior. Later I started lifting weights and abusing steroids. I was not concerned about the damaging effects the steroids would have on my body, only with the satisfaction they would give me now.

It was the same in business. I didn't care whom I had to step on to get to the top. I wanted to live for the *now*. I wanted a Ferrari *now*. I didn't care if I had to lie to get it.

Mom Accepts Jesus

There was another event that happened when I was nine that would later shape my life in a completely different way.

Much to the embarrassment of my Jewish family, my mother became a believer in Jesus. I wasn't even bar mitzvahed yet. I was going to Hebrew school twice a week. Both my sisters and I were actively involved in the temple.

Mom came home one evening and announced, "I've accepted Christ as my Lord and Savior." My father's first inclination was divorce, but he didn't do it. My mother's mother, my father's father, everyone in the family, including me, condemned my mother for this betrayal. We looked at anyone who would even mention the name of Christ as betraying their allegiance to God and committing the unpardonable sin.

It was nothing short of betrayal because we had our roots in Judaism on both sides of the family as far back as anyone could remember or document. There was just no logical explanation we knew of that would justify my mother accepting Jesus.

My dad only wanted to know one thing: what could a church give my mom that our temple and rabbi could not? My mother's answer was irrefutable. She replied, "I have a relationship, not a religion."

> **My dad only wanted to know one thing: what could a church give my mom that our temple and rabbi could not? My mother's answer was irrefutable. She replied, "I have a relationship, not a religion."**

From her youth, my mother had always been very goal oriented, always feeling that she had to perform. Her wealthy parents constantly demanded performance, performance, performance.

In Judaism she found the same pressures to perform. She had to keep the commandments and the 613 Levitical laws because God, the righteous disciplinarian, looks down upon us, waiting for us to perform. What my mother found through the Messiah was a God who accepted her the way she was, flaws and all. He did not demand performance, but rather gave her grace and mercy, concepts that were foreign to her in Judaism. Grace, because God was giving her something that she didn't deserve. And mercy, because God was withholding from her what she *did* deserve. Those two words transformed her life. No longer was she required to perform, perform, perform, struggling to fulfill all the requirements of the law. Instead, the law was fulfilled for her in the person and work of Jesus the Messiah, giving her life a whole new meaning.

> **...the law was fulfilled for her in the person and work of Jesus the Messiah, giving her life a whole new meaning.**

Dad forbade Mom to witness to the children. As a believer in the Messiah, she wanted to be obedient to her husband, so she complied. But her lifestyle changed. No longer was she emotionally bankrupt. After she accepted

Jesus, she treated the rest of the family with more patience and love. It was a radical change. She preached all the time and never used words.

Sixteen-Year-Old Entrepreneur

I was 16 years old when I started ZZZZ Best out of my parents' garage. It was never my original intention to defraud Wall Street. At 16 I just wanted to be recognized in school. I wasn't the best athlete, and I wasn't tremendously good looking. Many people in our high schools are not the star cheerleaders or the star football players. They are caught somewhere in between, looking for acceptance. That was me. Today you see kids trying to get acceptance through sexual promiscuity, alcohol, and drugs. I tried to gain acceptance by doing something that nobody else had done.

I started on a shoestring budget, working after school and on weekends. I hired a crew to do the cleaning jobs while I was at school. I hired my mother and another lady to set up the appointments. While everybody was worried about the algebra test on Friday, I was worried about how I was going to meet my payroll.

It was very challenging, but it gained me recognition. I was immediately put in the newspapers and on television. I was the first person anyone knew of to start a business at such a young age. To ensure greater exposure for myself and my new company, I again resorted to deception. Disguising my voice, I called a television station, pretending I was a ZZZZ Best customer. I went on and on about a

16-year-old who owned his own company and had just cleaned my carpets in between his algebra and Spanish classes. I suggested that the station do a story about this enterprising young man. Shortly afterward, I received a call from the station to arrange an interview.

When the television piece aired, I got addicted to the recognition again. I felt so good every time I got recognized that it eased the pain of my guilt about the wrong things I was doing to keep the company running. Because I wasn't old enough to have a checking account, I made a deal with a local liquor store owner who cashed my customers' checks and converted them into money orders for me to pay my bills. The owner had been a very good friend of mine ever since I was a little boy. He trusted me.

One day when I couldn't meet payroll, I should have said, "I'd better quit while I'm ahead. I gave it a try. I should just close up the company." Instead I stole some money orders from my friend. I was too addicted to the publicity and the recognition to let a lack of funds stand in my way.

> **I was too addicted to the publicity and the recognition to let a lack of funds stand in my way.**

Although it was stealing—plain and simple—I rationalized in my mind that it was for a good purpose and that I would pay the money back. Years later when I lied to banks to secure multi-million dollar loans, I again rationalized that I was going to pay them back and nobody was going to get hurt. It was for a good cause—I wasn't going to take the money and run to Europe. I'll make good on it, and then I'll stop this behavior, I promised myself.

Lies Upon Lies

One day I stole some jewelry from my grandmother to meet payroll. She had come over to our house, realized she forgot something, and asked if I could go back to her house and get it for her. While I was there, I went into her jewelry box and took some jewelry. I got $300 for it at a hocking place and deposited the money into my account to cover payroll that week. My grandmother knew it was me. At first I denied it. But she had seen the jewelry before she left. She was contemplating wearing it. When she got back, it was gone. The only person who had been in her apartment was me. Still, I denied it.

Later, though, I confessed, paid her back the money that she had said it was worth, and apologized to her. I felt terrible because my grandmother had helped me financially with the business.

While my grandmother forgave me, the whole incident showed how far I had fallen. What had been unthinkable when I first started the business was now standard procedure.

Compromise is subtle. It creeps up on you, and then when consequences don't immediately follow your actions, you compromise more. What starts out as lying on your tax return ends up with lying on multi-million dollar loans. That is the pattern. Compromise slowly leads to destruction.

> **Compromise is subtle. It creeps up on you, and then when consequences don't immediately follow your actions, you compromise more.**

I even faked robberies. When payroll got tight again, I was tired of temporary fixes; I wanted a big score. I staged a robbery at my office, called the insurance company, and said, "We just got robbed. All my equipment was taken." After a police report had been duly filed, I received a check to replace the "stolen" equipment.

I did that two or three times with various insurance companies, staging robberies in various stores, another progression of compromise.

Through these various activities, I raised enough extra money to open new stores and hire new employees. I was convinced that I had a just cause. But there was no excuse for what I was doing. Even though I wrapped it in some kind of justifiable garb, it was still nothing less than robbery and thievery.

Organized Crime

My uncle, a developer, one day asked me to go repair some carpets on a particular account. He said, "Barry, before you go in and do this job, I want you to know that the guy is a real Mafioso. Be careful."

Rather than be scared, my only thought as a young kid struggling in business was, *I know what the mob does. They give high-interest loans to people like me.* I looked at the job as an opportunity to raise capital for my company.

I wasn't worried because, up to that time, I had always figured out a way to pay off my loans. Also, I was convinced that since I was young and in the media, I would have a little extra grace period with the mob or whoever loaned me money.

I went voluntarily, eyes open, into a relationship with this particular individual. I told him about my financial difficulties, and he was able to arrange some loans for me with very high interest. I'd borrow, pay back, borrow, pay back. I got more deeply involved with some more people, but it was always voluntarily.

Never was I hurt or threatened to do what I had to do. As long as I paid the bills, things were OK.

> **Fraud is never an end in itself; it's always a means to some kind of end.**

Fraud is never an end in itself; it's always a means to some kind of end. What I wanted to do was get that ultimate amount of money. When my company got to a particular size, I wanted to go public on Wall Street to get enough money equity wise to pay off the mobsters and all the others and clean up everything.

How Much Is God?

At the height of my success, my mother came to me one day and asked, "Is all that money going to buy you a ticket to Heaven? What about God?"

Without missing a beat, I responded, "How much is God? I'll buy Him."

Devastated, my mother left my office determined to pray for the demise of ZZZZ Best, even though both she and my father worked for me. She didn't care about her job. She wanted the company to fail because she saw it as the stumbling block between me and a real relationship with Jesus.

Within a year, the company fell apart.

Phony Projects and Inflated Stock Prices

Although ZZZZ Best at its peak had about 1,300 employees in 23 locations doing carpet, furniture, and drapery cleaning, the restoration part of the business was fictitious. I was claiming that we were doing multi-million dollar restorations on buildings that had been damaged by fire or water. But there were no such jobs.

These contracts were my way of raising money. I would take the projects to investors and say, "If you lend me $100,000, I'll be able to complete this job. It will pay $30,000 in interest on your money in a 90-day period, and you will get your principal back plus a nice $30,000 score for three months." Of course, the money I brought in went to pay off the investors from the previous "project" and to keep the company afloat—not to restore buildings.

Besides creating cash flow, the restoration projects also increased my income statement, which ultimately led to a rise in my stock value. As these "jobs" began to increase, they made ZZZZ Best appear to be 10 times larger than it actually was.

ZZZZ Best stock was trading as high as $18 a share in March and April of 1987, which made me worth over $120 million on paper. In several months I would be able to sell some of my own restricted stock, I planned to sell a million shares, get $18 million in equity and clean up everything. In the meantime, we were making arrangements to buy Key Serv, which was the authorized carpet cleaner for Sears across the country. Had the $40 million deal gone through, we would have owned Sears' rights and had a national company.

Collapse

Right before the deal was to close, the *Los Angeles Times* published an article exposing credit card fraud I had been involved in two to three years before. My initial thought was that as long as no one discovered the bigger fraud—the restoration projects—I could find a way to defuse the negative publicity. But the article caused those arranging the financing for the Key Serv deal to take a closer look at my company. Instead of giving me the assumption of innocence, they now had reason to assume my guilt. And when they began to dig, they found out ZZZZ Best was nothing more than a facade.

The story ran on May 22, 1987. That day will be etched in my memory forever. ZZZZ Best stock fell five points. I personally lost $6 million for every point the stock dropped. Everybody and every bank called their loans on me. My accounts were frozen. I had 1,300 employees who were counting on me. And a $40 million deal that I had worked so hard to secure was about to get canceled. I was losing everything as nearly five years of work crumbled under my feet.

> **I was losing everything as nearly five years of work crumbled under my feet.**

The media that I was usually so good at persuading surrounded my office and asked me questions I couldn't answer. After I made a statement regarding the credit card allegations, my biggest fears were realized. One reporter said, "We understand that you say you completed a $7 million restoration job in Sacramento." Someone had actually gone to Sacramento to check. He continued, "We have found that there was no such job. What do you have to say for yourself?"

I knew it was over then. I knew it in my head, even though I didn't want to admit it. I fought like crazy to try to salvage things and persuaded people to lie to save the deal, but failure was inevitable.

Had the deal gone through, I would have gained that equity money. From a fraud standpoint I would have had things covered. But I believe it would only have been a matter of time before I committed fraud again because my heart wasn't changed.

Guilty and Lonely

In July 1987, shortly after I had resigned from the company in disgrace, the press surrounded my parents' house. *USA Today* and all the local news media were there to cover the huge story. This young entrepreneur, the youngest guy ever to begin a public company in the history of the United States, was a failure. I went over to see my mother to explain that she had no job anymore. Obviously, she knew that. She told me that she had been praying for the demise of ZZZZ Best since that day when I had offered to "buy" God. She said she loved me and that God's offer of grace and forgiveness was waiting for me in the person and work of Jesus. Then she said: "I know you don't want to talk to me about a lot of the things you did because it's uncomfortable for a mother and a son. My dear friend Dottie loves the Lord, and I would love for you to go talk to her."

My first thought was, *I don't need this Jesus stuff.* But Dottie was a long-time friend, and I was feeling so guilty and lonely. I wanted somebody to talk to, someone with whom I could be totally honest. I finally agreed.

> "I just have one question for you. Did it work? Did all the money, power, prestige, and fame bring any lasting meaning, contentment, or peace into your life?"

When I went to see Dottie, she said, "Barry, I'm not going to preach to you. I'm not going to tell you what this verse says or that verse. I just have one question for you. Did it work? Did all the money, power, prestige, and fame bring any lasting meaning, contentment, or peace into your life?"

I thought about my bankrupt life and replied, "No, it didn't."

She said, "I have the solution for you. It's the person and work of Jesus the Messiah. He is going to offer you complete forgiveness right now and freedom from guilt. He will even give you the strength to make it through the consequences of your actions."

She made two more key points: "Once you squeeze the toothpaste out of the tube, you can't put it back in," meaning that I couldn't change what I had done with ZZZZ Best. "But," she said, "it's never too late to start doing what's right."

> "But," she said, "it's never too late to start doing what's right."

That advice affected me profoundly. The irony of the whole ZZZZ Best scandal is that *I* was ultimately the one who got conned—by believing that making it to the top at the expense of my integrity and character was somehow going to bring peace, meaning, and contentment to my life. I bought the lie that it was OK to step on whomever I had to as long as I was getting to the top because that would bring me happiness. Instead, it brought me a life without meaning.

A week later I was walking along the beach. The news articles were bombarding me every day, saying I was going to spend the rest of my life in prison. As I walked alone that evening, I cried and asked Jesus to forgive me and to be my Lord and Savior.

While my prayer was sincere, in the back of my mind, I was thinking, *Maybe this will be my last great con. I'll just accept Jesus and hopefully get off with a light sentence.*

Old Habits Die Hard

Shortly after that experience, I did a *60 Minutes* interview on the advice of my lawyer. I had no intention of telling the truth, but saw it as a chance to prove my "innocence." It was horrible. Diane Sawyer was well prepared. She said, "It's true, is it not, Mr. Minkow, that you're involved with organized crime?"

And I said, "No, it's not true."

She said, "Well, can you explain this piece of paper?" And she produced the articles of incorporation for a company that had my name as president and as vice-president one of the mobsters. I claimed that someone had forged my signature.

Even though Jesus had forgiven me, it took a while for the Holy Spirit to really transform my life a little at a time. Suddenly, though, I began to see that I wasn't able to lie as

I had before. My conscience began to bother me even more than it used to.

Right after the *60 Minutes* interview, I ended up in the hospital with pneumonia and facing charges that could get me up to 270 years in prison. John Orr, one of the FBI agents, called me. He had been investigating me for six months and was about to indict me, but he wanted to know if I was OK because he knew I was abusing steroids and that was the reason for the pneumonia. He said, "I have to keep my professional distance from you, but it isn't anything personal. You did things wrong, and we're going to indict you for them. But we don't want you to die."

> **That really touched me, and I prayed right then to the Lord for a second chance and for forgiveness.**

That really touched me, and I prayed right then to the Lord for a second chance and for forgiveness.

Conviction, Sentencing, Prison

In late 1988 I was found guilty on all counts of fraud. The sentence: 26 years and $26 million. Everybody was there watching Barry get what he deserved. It was probably the most embarrassing moment of my life. The room was full of media and even the victims of the crime.

I had told my mother not to come, but she insisted. After the sentence was announced, there was a commotion in the courtroom, with reporters rushing to the phones to call in their stories. The marshals came and tried to whisk me back to my holding cell, but I stopped right as I was walking out of the courtroom to look back at my mother to see if she was crying and distraught. I had to know. She looked at me eye-to-eye, put her hands together, put them to her face, and lifted them upward as she smiled. Her actions spoke plainly: Jesus is in control; I'm not worried a bit.

That image gave me the strength not just to do my time, but to leave prison different from the way I came.

I served a little over seven years in prison.

Sometimes I was asked whether my profession of faith was just "jail house religion" and another con. When I was in prison I wrote all my victims and told them I wanted to pay them back. Many of them said, "Let's see what you say when you are released and you don't have to use us to get out of prison."

I'll never forget in 1989, after I had been in prison for two years, I was baptized in a bathtub by the pastor there along with three witnesses from the outside. When I was done I was standing there dripping wet. Before handing me a towel, the pastor asked, "Do you have anything to say?"

> **"Lord, can you please make this real? Because I've been a liar and a con man all my life. I don't even know if I'm lying and conning right now. I just pray that if Jesus exists that my experience will be real."**

The witnesses later said their lives were impacted by my response. I said, "Lord, can you please make this real? Because I've been a liar and a con man all my life. I don't even know if I'm lying and conning right now. I just pray that if Jesus exists that my experience will be real."

In less than five years I finished my bachelor's and master's degrees in systematic theology and became president of the Fellowship of Christian Athletes in the facility. The Lord had responded to my prayer and made Jesus a reality in my life.

Comeback

I've been out of prison since December 1994. Legally, I don't have to go out of my way to pay back my victims. I could get a regular job and pay a minimal amount each year. But I'm channeling all my time and energy into legitimate means to try to pay them back. All the proceeds from my book about my experiences are going to the victims. When I do fraud prevention seminars, a material amount of whatever I earn goes to them.

Some of the victims have become my best friends. The very FBI agents who put me in prison asked me to speak at their bank day seminar. These people were my biggest skeptics and critics.

The greatest con in life is to believe that there is no eternity, no Jesus. But Jesus *does* exist. He is the only one who rose from the dead, came back, and verified that there is an eternity to be gained—or lost. Embracing Jesus by faith will transform your life in ways you never thought possible.

Commentary by Sid Roth

I was a pretty good person. After all, I had never robbed any banks or murdered anyone. In other words, compared to most people, I was good—or was I?

God says, "There is none who does good" (Ps. 14:1 NKJV). This is why He gave us the ten commandments. They allow us to evaluate our goodness by God's standards.

It is a sin to have sex outside of marriage. It is a sin to tell a lie, even a "white" lie. It is a sin to covet. I used to covet my friends' wives, money, and jobs. It is a sin to steal. I cheated on my expense accounts. I had not honored my mother or father. And I certainly valued the god of "self" more than the God of creation. Some place work or money or sports or sex above God. He calls this idolatry. According to Torah standards, even just one sin will separate us from God forever. We will all stand before God on Judgment Day. We all are guilty of sin. We all deserve punishment.

God's mercy according to His Law is our only salvation. During Temple days, God accepted the blood of innocent lambs as a covering for our sin. Today, God's Law requires the blood of Jesus. Thank God my sins are forgiven. I have repented. And because of Messiah's blood, I do not have to face God's wrath.

CHAPTER 3
BY ROSE PRICE

CHAPTER 3

The Survivor

I am a survivor of Hitler's Holocaust. My family, who lived in a little city in Poland, was warm and caring. We looked out for one another. My relatives lived within walking distance of each other, so if it rained and you ducked into the nearest house, you were always in the home of a cousin or an aunt or uncle.

My upbringing was very Orthodox. My mother instilled in me that Judaism was life. I never knew a difference between a high holiday or a low holiday. A holiday was a holiday. Every *Shabbat* (Sabbath) was even celebrated as a holiday.

My mother and my grandmother would start getting ready for the Shabbat on Wednesday, baking *challa* (bread). On Friday they prepared the fish and the chicken soup and made the noodles. In the afternoon we would take a *cholent*—a one-pot dish with meat, vegetables, and potatoes—to the baker to cook.

We would take special baths and dress in our finest clothes. The table was all set in beautiful white linen and whatever silver we had.

Meal time was family time. On Friday nights we had fish. Father would come home from the synagogue and recite the *Kiddish*, the blessing over the wine and the *challa*; then he would bless the children.

Saturday morning we would go to the synagogue. After services, we would stop by the bakery and bring home the *cholent*. We all sat around grandmother's table and enjoyed the Sabbath meal.

The Nazi Horror

When Hitler took power, change came quickly. The Germans invaded in September 1939. One day at school shortly after the invasion, all the Jewish students were called up to the front of the classroom. With a guard standing nearby, our teacher told us, "Don't come back to the school anymore because you are Jews." I was ten and one-half years old. We were all absolutely devastated.

The next thing the Germans did was throw us out of our home and force us to live in a ghetto. They took the whole town of Jews and put us on one street.

My sister, who is two years older, and I were among the first to be sent away. We were on our way to visit our grandmother when the Germans grabbed us and put us to work in the ammunition factory.

It was a horror because we went from a warm house into freezing conditions, and from a loving, hugging, kissing family to a man constantly beating us with a whip. For a while we went back to our parents in the evenings. But one day, instead of letting us return home, they marched us into the woods. That summer I had been in the woods gathering mushrooms, blueberries, and raspberries. Now I was confined to a prison camp in those same woods.

> **That summer I had been in the woods gathering mushrooms, blueberries, and raspberries. Now I was confined to a prison camp in those same woods.**

It's unthinkable what those people did to us. It's almost indescribable. In the morning, they woke us up when it was still dark. We had to go outside, no matter what the weather was, and line up five deep for them to count us.

We worked a full day at the factory. I operated a machine that stretched out a piece of aluminum from a quarter of an inch to the length of a rifle bullet. I had to grease it, feed it, and take away the shells.

Before the invasion, my biggest responsibilities were to go to school, learn, come home, help my mother with the housework, do some gardening, and watch out for my younger sister. Now I was being told that either I learned how to work that machine or I would die. And I had to learn quickly.

I cried for a while, until one day I just couldn't cry anymore because I didn't have any tears left. That happened after the city was evacuated, and I knew I would never again see my parents or my family. That was my last day of crying for 25 years.

> **I prayed, and nothing happened.**
> **When my prayers were not answered,**
> **I concluded that there was no God.**

At first I would still pray. I would get up in the morning and say the *Modeh Ani,* and during the day I would say the *Shema* and just pray to God. One day I prayed that God would send my mother because I was hungry and homesick. I needed a mother's hug instead of the beatings. I wanted to take a bath because I was covered with dirt and we didn't have soap. I prayed, and nothing happened. When my prayers were not answered, I concluded that there was no God.

The Concentration Camps

I was transferred from one concentration camp to another until I was sent to Bergen-Belsen and then Dachau. It's hard for me to believe that I lived through such horror. Such horrible, horrible things happened at Bergen-Belsen. We were tortured. We were put in a field and forced to dig sugar beets out of the almost frozen ground with our bare hands. I remember my hands bleeding badly.

We had many difficult experiences in the camps. One stands out as particularly cruel. I was working in the field one day digging up sugar beets, and by then I was more like a zombie because I had been in these conditions for several years. I decided I was going to steal a sugar beet and eat it. I was determined that my belly was not going to hurt that night.

All we used to receive was a quarter-of-an-inch thick piece of bread—it was 80 percent sawdust—and a cup of coffee. That was our food for 24 hours. Obviously, this was barely enough food to exist on, let alone to sustain someone working in the extreme cold.

When the guard caught me, I got such a bad beating that even today when I talk about it I can still feel the cat-o'-nine tails on my back and on my face and around my body and the punishment of hanging by my hands—all because I stole a sugar beet.

One time while we were lined up, we were completely undressed for an experiment to see how long it would take for our blood to freeze.

The cold weather alone killed many of us because we were not dressed properly. We would have to stand in line for hours, no matter how deep the snow was, half naked and without shoes.

One time while we were lined up, we were completely undressed for an experiment to see how long it would take for our blood to freeze. To this day, when I am in cold weather, and my toes and fingers go completely numb, I remember that time when my body started to freeze. The only reason I survived the experiment was because several people fell on top of me and their bodies kept me warm.

I had made up my mind that I would survive the same day that I had said there was no God. When I did survive, I took full credit. Later, I realized it had to have been the Lord.

But there were days when I thought I wasn't going to make it. When we were on our way to Dachau, our train was bombed. As we ran into the woods to get away from the train, I thought to myself, *That's it. I've made enough bullets. Let them use the bullets on me.* Death looked better than life.

One time when I was still in a camp in my own hometown, I was walking across the field with somebody, and I smiled. For the offense of smiling, the Germans put me in a sewer tank for 24 hours. I had to stay on my toes to keep from drowning. I was no more than 12 years old at the time.

> **For the offense of smiling, the Germans put me in a sewer tank for 24 hours. I had to stay on my toes to keep from drowning.**

Another difficult time was when my sister, who was in the same camp, got typhoid fever. She was my last living family member, and I didn't think I could go on if I lost her too. The guards came in periodically to check for those who were sick. Then they would take them outside and leave them to freeze. I laid on top of my sister to protect her, and when they asked for people to lift up their hands to show they were healthy, I put my hand up in place of hers.

Selected to Be Shot

Twice, I was selected to be shot. Both times when the guards unlocked the chain, I ran away. The second time I ran into a guard. I was running so hard I bounced off of him. But he didn't see me. It could only have been God. If he had seen me, he would have shot me himself. I looked up at him and then fled into a wooded part of the camp.

When we were finally liberated in May 1945, I was full of unforgiveness for what I had been through. I hated the Germans with a passion. The unforgiveness literally poisoned my body, causing me to need 27 operations.

I was looking for somebody who would be willing to drop a bomb on Germany and Poland. I had lost all of my family except my sister and one aunt—nearly 100 relatives.

My New Life

After I was released, I came to America, got married, and had children. As much as I hated God, I became active in the traditional synagogue. My children needed to learn about Judaism, but I couldn't teach them because I was dead inside. Socially, I was the best Jew. I was active in helping to build the Hebrew school. I even worked my way up to become president of the sisterhood.

If someone had asked me back then, "Do you believe in God?" I would have said, "No." Even today many rabbis don't believe in the Bible, and very few believe in God. But I believed in maintaining my Jewish identity and tradition.

My Daughter Believes in Jesus

One day my teenage daughter came to me and said the worst thing I could imagine. She said, "Mommy, I believe in Jesus Christ, and He is the Jewish Messiah." I nearly had a heart attack. I told her what Jesus Christ did to her family and why she didn't have many aunts and uncles. The Nazi guards had told me over and over that because I killed Jesus Christ, He hated me and put me into the camps to kill me.

> **She said, "Mommy, I believe in Jesus Christ, and He is the Jewish Messiah."**

When I was seven or eight years old, I was hit in the head with a crucifix by a priest in Poland for the "crime" of walking on the sidewalk in front of his church.

So for my daughter to believe in Jesus Christ was death. I threw her out. I couldn't have this enemy living in my house. When my husband went to the house where she was staying to check on her, he became a believer too. The house was used as an outreach to Jewish people.

My younger daughter was still going to a private Hebrew school. But somehow I knew that she had secretly become a Messianic believer, and I beat her for it, even though I don't remember doing it.

> **I had lost my first family under Hitler, and now was about to lose my second family, all because of this Jesus. I was ready to meet Jesus and kill Him.**

After my husband accepted the Lord, he came home and started reading Proverbs 31 to me. I didn't know what Proverbs 31 was, but when he told me he believed also, he became a traitor to me too. The rabbi couldn't do anything with him. He was very stubborn. I was ready to leave my family, but I couldn't. A friend of mine, a lawyer, said, "If you leave the house, the authorities will put you in jail for desertion of your minor children."

I had lost my first family under Hitler, and now was about to lose my second family, all because of this Jesus. I was ready to meet Jesus and kill Him.

I tried everything possible to reach both children. For the first time I told them about the concentration camps. I begged them. I pleaded with them to reject this Jewish enemy. For two thousand years we had been persecuted because this man was supposed to be a Messiah. I told them everything I had learned, and nothing helped.

Since my husband had become a believer, he insisted that my daughter come back home. They witnessed to me

THEY THOUGHT FOR THEMSELVES

constantly. I would find my Jewish Bible opened and little pieces of paper with Scriptures on it.

I didn't know they were Scriptures because I didn't know the Bible.

I Go to the Rabbi

I ran to the rabbi. He would tell me different Scriptures with which to challenge my family. In response, they would give me five more.

At the urging of my family, I asked the rabbi about Isaiah 53. He said, "No Jew reads that, especially a Jewish woman." So I couldn't read it. The same with Psalm 22. There are 328 prophecies of the coming of the suffering servant Messiah. I asked the rabbi about almost all of them. Finally, the rabbi told me not to come to the synagogue anymore because I had read him Isaiah 53.

I kept yelling and screaming and crying, "Help me! I'm not going that way. What do you want from me? My family is dead because they believe in Jesus, you tell me, but my food disappears. Who is eating the food? Why do I have so much laundry? If they are all dead, then why is it? Help me!"

> **I started sneaking down to the basement and reading the New Testament in a locked room.**

He just replied, "No. I can't help you anymore."

So I started sneaking down to the basement and reading the New Testament in a locked room. I read Matthew first, and it showed me Jesus was a gentle man. He wasn't a killer of my people, but a very gentle man. Then I started to think about what I believed.

I went to another rabbi for help, but he said, "Look, I can't help you because I don't read the Bible very much."

The Millionaire

Shortly after that encounter I went to a dinner at Arthur DeMoss' house. Mr. DeMoss was a wealthy Christian businessman who would open his home once a year as an outreach to Jewish people. He asked me if I would mind if he prayed for me. I told him, "I don't care if you stand on your head. It's your house." Instead of standing on his head, he started to pray. Jews never close their eyes in prayer, but all of a sudden I closed my eyes and said a very simple prayer:

> God of Abraham, Isaac, and Jacob, if it's true, if He who they are saying is Your Son, and You have a Son, and He is really the Messiah, OK. But, Father, if He isn't, forget that I talked to You.

That was the first prayer I had prayed since 1942. I felt the biggest stone rolling off my back. For the first time since the war, I cried, and I felt so clean. I knew He was real, and I made Him *my* Messiah.

> **For the first time since the war, I cried, and I felt so clean. I knew He was real, and I made Him *my* Messiah.**

When Holocaust survivors get angry with me today because I am a Messianic Jew, I just show love to them because I know how they feel. I've been there. I don't argue with them.

Berlin Calls

One day I got a call from Sid Roth. A friend of his, a pastor from a large church in Berlin, had just called him to say, "We're going to rent the largest coliseum in Berlin, the one that Hitler used for his meetings, and we're looking for Messianic Jews to take part in the events we have planned."

Sid said, "I have the perfect person," meaning me. But when he called me, I refused.

When I left Germany I swore I would never, ever go back to that accursed land. And here he was asking me to go back to Germany. *How could he?* For six months I wrestled about whether to go. I asked the Lord to kill me, to take me home, but not to send me back because as soon as I started praying, the word came, "Yes, you have to go back, and you have to forgive."

I finally surrendered. I went with my husband and four other believers. Many more came later. It was, as I said, a six-month struggle. I had people pray and fast for me.

This was a big event. A number of prominent Christians were there including Pat Robertson, Demos Shakarian, and Pat Boone.

When I walked into that coliseum, the one where Hitler said the Nazis would rule the world for a thousand years, it was jam packed with young Germans. A number of them had stars of David, Jewish stars, around their necks. Israeli flags were waving.

When I saw the American leaders, some of whom I knew, and I saw the German people wearing stars of David and mezuzahs, I thought, *It's impossible.* Then I thought, *What am I doing here? Lord, what do you want from me? Get me out of here. I don't want to speak German. Am I doing this right, or am I telling the Germans and the world that it's OK to go kill Jews?* These thoughts tormented me until I spoke.

Confronted by Nazis

On Sunday they called me up to speak. I don't remember saying the things that were printed. I don't remember speaking on forgiveness. But after I finished my talk, some people came up to me who were the last people on the face of this earth that I wanted to see. They were ex-Nazis. Apparently, I had asked for any ex-Nazis to come up and be prayed for and forgiven. I don't remember saying it, but here they were asking me to forgive them. Could I forgive them face-to-face as I had from the podium?

That's when I realized that I had spoken on forgiveness. One of those who had come forward was a guard from

Dachau. He had been in charge of punishment. When he came and identified himself, my body shriveled up in pain as he knelt down. He was pleading with me to forgive him.

I am a believer, but people cannot comprehend what I experienced in Dachau and Bergen-Belsen. They cannot imagine the hell I went through. It was only by the grace of God that I was able to forgive those who came forward, because Rose Price could not forgive them for the atrocities I went through as a child.

> ...one of the ex-Nazis whom I had prayed with for forgiveness came up to me. He said that after I had prayed with him he had his first night's sleep since the war.

As I was ready to leave Berlin, one of the ex-Nazis whom I had prayed with for forgiveness came up to me. He said that after I had prayed with him he had his first night's sleep since the war.

Show Me the Strength

Another time I was in Germany again, and I realized I was not far from Bergen-Belsen. I knew that I had to go back. Once and for all I had to bury Bergen-Belsen. I had a Swedish couple with me, Susan and Gary, and a German man named Otto—all believers.

I had to ask a guide for the location of the main gate. I didn't recognize it because the barracks had all been burned. But I knew if they put me where the main gate had been, I could find where the barracks had stood. I was amazed that even today no grass grows where the electric wires were located. No matter how many times they plant grass, it does not grow. The guide gave me a list of the names of those who had been at Bergen-Belsen, and I found my sister's and my name on the list. We were on the last transport out from Bergen-Belsen to Dachau. After that, all those who remained died of typhus.

I cried, and I wept. At one point I was hollering at Bergen-Belsen, "You died, but I survived! I am here! I survived!"

While I was hollering, I started to pray for the salvation of the country and that the German people would learn of the Messiah's love and forgiveness.

At one point I asked, "Lord, how can I pray that prayer at this cemetery where so much happened to me, so much that is indescribable?"

As I was praying, the German man became hysterical. I went over to him to hug him, and he said, "How can you pray for us when we did that to you? My family was involved with this. We put you here. How can you? Show me the strength. Show me the strength." Then he asked for forgiveness, and the four of us just kept on crying and praying for one another and for the German people.

You Have to Forgive

If you feel you cannot forgive someone, you cannot hate anyone more than I hated the Germans. I lost my stomach. I had 27 operations before I went to Berlin. Hate has an address in your body. Love cannot dwell in the body with hate. When I finally gave up all the hate and love started coming in, something happened inside my body. I didn't have pain anymore. I haven't had an operation since 1981 because the Lord has taken all that poison out of me.

> **Nobody knows the pain you have gone through, and nobody knows the pain I went through. But there is no excuse for hate. You have to forgive.**

Nobody knows the pain you have gone through, and nobody knows the pain I went through. But there is no excuse for hate. You have to forgive. You have to give up the hate.

It's not even up to you to have the strength to forgive. You cannot do anything in your own power. You have to go to the Lord, and the Lord will give you the strength.

Commentary by Sid Roth

What kind of power could allow Rose Price to forgive Nazis who tortured and murdered almost her entire family?

This power is the Holy Spirit of God. God predicts a day will come in which He will change man's heart and give him a new spirit: "I will give you a new heart, and a new spirit will I put within you;

and I will remove the heart of stone out of your body..." (Ezek. 36:26).

This new Spirit that God will put within us will allow us to live at a higher level and overcome all fears. Jeremiah 31:30,33 (31,34 in some versions), written hundreds of years before the birth of Jesus, predicts a new covenant from God that will not only cause God to remember our sins no more, but allow us to *know* Him!

Imagine having intimacy with God. You can hear His voice. You can experience His love. I know this is true because I know Him. And what He has done for me, He desires to do for you.

CHAPTER 4
BY ALYOSHA RYABINOV

CHAPTER 4

A New Song

I was born to Jewish parents in Kiev in 1958. My parents tried to hide our Jewishness. There was nothing Jewish in our home, and we never attended synagogue. Yet even as a child, I wanted to be Jewish because my mother and father were. I couldn't rationalize it, but it just felt right inside.

As I grew up, the only religion I was exposed to was atheism. Atheism was taught in the former Soviet Union as the truth. In college they even offered a course on it in which they ridiculed people who believed in God. When my professor claimed that science had proven one hundred times over that there is no God, I wanted to ask for even one proof out of a hundred. I didn't feel atheism was based on any scientific proof. But I didn't have the courage to voice my inner thoughts.

I Knew There Was a God

I somehow knew there was a God. I knew that even something as simple as a wristwatch could never have been constructed through random acts of chance. How could all those tiny pieces of metal have assembled themselves together over millions of years? Only a fool would believe that.

If a wristwatch could not have evolved, how could they ever expect me to believe that something as complicated as a human being just "happened"? Even one cell in the human body is much more complex than a watch. People have to be blind to deny the existence of a Creator.

I come from a family of musicians. My grandfather was a violinist and composer. My father was a violinist. My mother is a classical guitarist. They were well known in the former Soviet Union. My father even played in the orchestra, which was a great accomplishment since Jews were discriminated against. When I was five years old, I began to study piano at music school. I didn't know how good I was until I entered a few competitions in the fifth and sixth grades. To my surprise, I won the first prize twice. After I finished music school and decided I was going to be a professional musician, I practiced between six and eight hours a day at least six days a week.

I appeared to be on my way to a promising career, except for one thing—I was Jewish. In the Soviet Union, that was a major drawback. When a Jewish person wanted to enter college or pursue a career, it was much harder for him simply because he was Jewish. In spite of the odds, I did manage to gain admission to college and earn my bachelor's degree.

The next step for me would have been to attend the conservatory. I was talented enough to get in, but at that time my grandfather emigrated to the United States. This was in 1979 before large numbers were allowed to leave. Now I had two strikes against me: I was Jewish and the grandson of a "traitor." My grandfather was a well-known art critic. Because the circles of music and art are so closely aligned, everyone in music knew that my grandfather now lived in a capitalist country. As a result, they would never accept me into the conservatory.

The Long Wait

At that point, I wanted to get out of the country so badly I didn't care where I went. Of course, the authorities made the process very difficult. I don't know of one person during that time who was allowed to emigrate without great challenges. You are required to gather numerous documents, some of which are ridiculous. For example, a friend of mine who was divorced for many years had to get a document from his former wife saying that she would allow him to leave.

In the office where I submitted the documents, they called me a traitor. I was prepared for the verbal abuse, but it wasn't pleasant. I didn't feel I had betrayed my country. I believed every person should have a choice where to live.

After I turned in all the documents, I had to wait. Some people were forced to wait for years. Eventually, someone calls you and tells you whether you can go or not. But the waiting period is very difficult. I couldn't work because I had applied for permission to emigrate and no one would hire me. And now the army wanted to draft me. They do that to bring more fear and harassment.

When I had waited for about eight months, I started to get very anxious. I learned that in some cases people were denied permission to emigrate. I became very fearful. I thought, *What if they don't let me leave? If that happens I can never establish myself as a musician in Russia.* I would always be persecuted. People would always know that I had tried to "escape" from Russia, and my future life would be full of misery.

> **I needed to pour out my heart to someone, but I didn't feel there was any human who could possibly help me. So I thought, if there were a God in Heaven, I should try Him.**

I needed to pour out my heart to someone, but I didn't feel there was any human who could possibly help me. So I thought, if there were a God in Heaven, I should try Him. The question was, Where do I find Him? My first instinct was to go to a synagogue, but I didn't know where any were. And you don't want to walk around the streets of the Soviet

Union asking, "Where's the nearest synagogue?" If the person you talk to is KGB, you might end up in prison.

So I decided to go to a church instead. The one I found happened to be Russian Orthodox. As I walked inside, I got confused by all the pictures of saints on the walls. There were so many, I didn't know which one to pray to. As I walked around the church, I saw a replica of Jesus (Yeshua is His Hebrew name) on the cross. My atheism class helped me because I had learned that Jesus is for the Christians. Of course they taught that He never existed, even as a man. I certainly didn't know anything about all the saints pictured there. So I decided to pray to Jesus. I said, "Jesus, please get me out of this country." Then I turned around and left.

Our family received permission to emigrate soon after that. But I forgot about the prayer. We emigrated in 1979 to Chicago. Right away I started to study music at DePaul University.

Now that I was in a free country, I wanted to investigate my Jewish roots. I began to read about Jewish history. I even went to a reformed synagogue a few times. Although I was a bit bored with the service, I was excited to be among my people. My heritage had been withheld from me for so long, it was like getting back something that had been stolen. I also got involved at a Jewish community center.

I Find the Messiah

One thing I learned was that Christians and Jews do not mix. I never knew that before. My atheism course had taught me a little about different religions, but I didn't know that Jews were told not to accept Jesus as their Messiah.

> **One day my sister came home and told our mother she believed in God and that Jesus was the Jewish Messiah. Mom didn't take it very well.**

One day my sister came home and told our mother she believed in God and that Jesus was the Jewish Messiah. Mom didn't take it very well. As they discussed the matter, I listened from another room. To my surprise, what my sister said made sense to me. That was a miracle in itself, because I never gave much weight to anything she had to say.

Quietly, without telling anyone, I began to read books about Jesus that my sister had brought home. One book was about several rabbis who had found the Messiah. That was stunning to me. I was totally amazed that a rabbi could believe in Jesus. The book also discussed prophecies of the Bible that had been fulfilled. I was fascinated by passages such as Isaiah 53, which contained so many Messianic prophecies.

I wanted to know the truth. So I asked God to give me a sign if Jesus really was the Messiah. Suddenly, a bright light came into my room. It stayed for a little while, and then it left. But even after God had answered my prayer for emigration to the U.S. and now had sent this supernatural light, I was still not willing to admit to anyone what I was beginning to believe. I had grown up in such unbelief that I asked God for another sign, but I didn't get any more.

My sister attended Bible studies with a group that met right in the midst of the Jewish community. My mother feared that my sister would be persecuted for believing in Jesus and asked her not to go back. But my sister said, "I really want to study the Bible. Can the group come to our house?" Since our house was not close to the Jewish community center, my mother agreed. When the group arrived for their meeting, they invited me to join them. I wanted to, but I still didn't want to admit it. I said, "I'm not interested, but I'll sit and listen." During the course of the Bible study, the leader suddenly pointed to me and asked, "Do you believe that Yeshua is the Messiah?" Immediately, I was going to respond, "No," but I couldn't. Instead, a new-found strength welled up within me, and I said, "Yes." By the time I told my mother, she had grown more accustomed to the idea. It didn't matter that much to her whether we believed in Jesus or not. She was just afraid of persecution from the traditional Jewish community.

> **By the time I told my mother, she had grown more accustomed to the idea. It didn't matter that much to her whether we believed in Jesus or not. She was just afraid of persecution from the traditional Jewish community.**

When I finished my master's degree program at DePaul University, I gave two recitals. They were the best achievements of my life. For the two hours that I played the concerts and for a short time afterward, I felt a great sense of accomplishment. People really loved the performances and praised me. But by the following day, I felt empty. All those hours of daily practice year after year had yielded only a couple brief moments of glory. Now the glory was gone, and all that was left was this strange, empty feeling. At first, I wanted to produce and play more great music so people would lift me up again and tell me I was wonderful. Otherwise, I felt I would sink. It's natural to desire to be great, but we are not to use it to bring glory to ourselves. The Lord showed me He wanted me to live my whole life for Him. So for a year I didn't play piano. And for about two years, I didn't give any significant concerts. Piano was an idol for me. I put my idol on the altar and said, "If you don't want me to use this for the rest of my life, I won't. I want my life to magnify You, God."

In the meantime, I attended Moody Bible Institute, where I met my wife, Jody, who also is Jewish and believes in Yeshua. After one semester, we had an opportunity to go to Israel. A highlight of my time there was when I prayed for a boy with epilepsy. Jody and I went to see him with a Russian friend who had just become a believer in Jesus. It was difficult to communicate because we didn't share a common language. We spoke English and Russian and the boy's mother spoke Spanish and Hebrew. God showed me there was a demon causing the epilepsy. So for the first time in my life I told a demon to get out in the name of Jesus.

Suddenly, the boy indicated he felt something leave him. He did not know what I had prayed because he didn't understand the language. Months later I found out that he never had any more occurrences of epilepsy!

> God showed me there was a demon causing the epilepsy. ...I told a demon to get out in the name of Jesus. Suddenly, the boy indicated he felt something leave him.

Playing for God

After we returned from Israel, I began to understand that I was to use my talent for the piano to serve God. I also felt the desire to praise God with singing. That was interesting to me because I don't sing very well. Anyone who becomes a new believer can receive a new song, whether he is a musician or not. When that new song started to come out of me, I went to the piano and began to praise God. Some beautiful new music compositions came out of it.

God has continued in His faithfulness to me over the years. He has given me the opportunity to play in Sweden, Germany, Austria, Ukraine, Israel, and Canada, as well as the United States. I now have eight music recordings. And God has blessed Jody and me with two wonderful children, Josiah and Yasmine. Maybe you are experiencing great difficulties in your life as I did. I looked in many different directions for the answers. But I found that the only way to have true peace and victory is through knowing the Messiah. He will put a new song in your mouth.

Commentary by Sid Roth

Although most American Jews are agnostics, most Russian Jews are taught to be atheists. This is rapidly changing in both countries. Hundreds of thousands of Russian Jews like Alyosha are now believers in Jesus. And there are hundreds of Messianic Jewish synagogues in America to accommodate Jewish believers in Jesus.

Where do you stand? Do you believe there is a God who created the world? When I was in school, the theory of evolution sounded reasonable. Today, I realize it takes more faith to believe this complex universe evolved through chance than to believe the account of creation in the Bible.

Consider the example Alyosha gave of a wristwatch. If you took it completely apart and shook the pieces around in a box for a million years, would it come out reassembled and ticking? How much more complex is the heart and the thousands of miles of capillaries that help make up the circulatory system!

Did you know the human eye has one million nerve fibers in each optic nerve? Each one is connected to the brain. When the eye points at something, it sends a message to the brain that tells the brain the distance to the object. The brain then sends a message to the muscles of the lens telling it how much to change its curvature. In a split second, the object is in focus.

In the last 24 hours your heart has beat 100,000 times; your blood has traveled 186 million miles throughout 60,000 miles of tubing in your body. Your kidneys have filtered over 42 gallons of liquid. And you have probably exercised 7 million brain cells. No machine made by man compares with your body.

By the way, if man evolved from the monkey, why have we never found full fossils or animals that are part ape and part human? And why has *every* "missing link" between apes and men turned out to be a mistake or hoax?

I remember in high school we used to study the evolutionary date charts. They stated as fact that dinosaurs lived millions of years *before man*. At the Creation Evidences Museum in Glynn Rose, Texas, we can see evidence of *human and dinosaur footprints made within minutes of each other* captured in a limestone bed. Actually, this same limestone has 57 human footprints and 192 dinosaur prints—proof the evolutionary charts are fantasy. Man and dinosaurs lived on Earth together.

What about the "Big Bang" theory? If a big explosion created order out of chaos, why has every observable explosion in history brought disorder? The Bible says the real "big bang" is yet to come:

> *But the day of the Lord will come as a thief in the night, in which the heavens will pass away with a great noise, and the elements will melt with fervent heat; both the earth and the works that are in it will be burned up* (2 Peter 3:10 NKJV).

Then God will bring us a new heaven and a new earth. It will be in perfect order—a garden of Eden:

> *Now I saw a new heaven and a new earth, for the first heaven and the first earth had passed away* … (Revelation 21:1 NKJV).

CHAPTER 5
BY SHARON R. ALLEN

CHAPTER 5

Yiddishkeit

Ny life in 1982 was dedicated to the well-being of
my family and to my activities at Chabad of Irvine
Jewish Center. One can find Chabad centers in even the
most remote communities of the world. I have always had a
deep admiration for Chabad, and that is why my husband
and I supported the Chabad movement here in Southern
California.

But wait, I'm getting ahead of myself. I want to go back
to the beginning—my beginning.

I was born in 1945 at Beth Israel Hospital in New York
City. My Hebrew name is Sura Rifka. I was raised in an
observant Jewish home. From the moment my mom lit the
Shabbos (Sabbath) candles on Friday evening until one
hour after sundown on Saturday night, there were certain
rules and regulations that we followed. They did not make

us feel constricted or oppressed. It was our way of showing our love, our respect, and our devotion to God.

We followed the rabbinical injunctions, such as not using electricity on the Shabbos. We would leave one light on in the hall which was turned on before Shabbos started and was left on through the night and the next day until one hour after sundown Saturday night when Shabbos was over. We were not permitted to work on Shabbos, and that included my homework, since on Shabbos one is not allowed to write on, cut, or tear paper. We knew that the Shabbos was special because of what we did or did not do, and it was distinct from the other days of the week.

Of course, my mother kept a kosher kitchen where only kosher foods were permitted. Separate sets of dishes and utensils designated for *milchig* (dairy) or *fleishig* (meat) products were strictly enforced. My brother and I knew from the time we could reach up into the drawers and cabinets never to confuse those items deemed milchig and fleishig. Separate sets of dishes were also needed for Passover. Those dishes were brought out of the "hard-to-reach" top cabinet once a year to be used only on Pesach.

We observed all the Jewish holidays. My brother and I attended Hebrew School. We grew up knowing who we were within the Jewish Community.

Moving West

As a young adult, I married a man from a similar Jewish background. We had a daughter, whom we named Elisa.

Her Hebrew name is Chava Leah. When she was only a few years old, we divorced. We received a Jewish divorce, known as a *get*.

I worked in the "Garment Center" in New York City. During this time Elisa attended Jewish Day School. I remember those early years when Elisa and I would wait for her school bus on cold, snowy, dark winter mornings at seven o'clock. We would huddle together freezing in the wind. It was on such a morning when I whispered to my daughter, "There has got to be a better way."

Moving out of state seemed like a step in the right direction. Elisa had an allergy problem that was worse during the damp winter months. New York had the worst winter climate for children like her. I had heard a doctor on a talk show mention that when people with certain allergies moved to another climate, their allergies would often disappear. With that doctor's words echoing in my ears, I sat down and made a list of the leading Garment Centers in the country. The doctor's theory about the benefits of moving was certainly worth a try.

On August 27, 1974, Elisa and I arrived in Los Angeles, California. Almost immediately, I enrolled her in Yavneh Yeshiva because school was starting in September. She was six years old. We lived near the school in the Fairfax District, the Orthodox section of town, and became involved with the Shaari Tefillah Congregation.

In a few years, my parents moved to Los Angeles to join us, and shortly after that we moved south to Orange County. At that time there was a big real estate boom, and, like many others, I decided to get my real estate license. Once I received my license, I started to work in an office owned by a man named Ron Allen. He was to become my husband.

Business Was His Religion

When Ron and I first met, he knew I was Jewish and that I was raised in an observant Jewish home. All I knew about Ron's religious background was that he was a Protestant. He never mentioned Jesus, the New Testament, or church. If he had, I would have run in the opposite direction. Apparently, he hadn't been to church since he was a teenager. He was 42. I was 32. Religion was the furthest thing from Ron's mind; business was his religion.

As Ron got to know our Jewish traditions, he embraced them as his own and eagerly participated. Because of Ron's warm and loving ways, my parents welcomed him into the family. My mother would say about Ron, "He's so *hamisha*," which in Yiddish means, "He's so comfortable to be with."

We were active in Chabad and became attached to the rabbi, Mendel Duchman, whom we admired and respected. Part scholar, part showman, and part businessman, Rabbi Duchman was successful in renewing peoples' interest in the Jewish lifestyle. His wife Rochel was warm, caring, and knowledgeable. She was the picture of the young, Jewish *balaboosta* (conscientious, immaculate housewife), a *rebbetzen's rebbetzen* (rabbi's wife), so to speak.

Ron and I knew right away that this was where we belonged. I became very active in the Chabad women's group.

Converting to Judaism

A few years after Ron and I were married, our discussions about his converting to Judaism turned serious. I knew that our future together could be impaired if Ron refused. Having a Jewish home and raising Elisa Jewish was foremost in my mind. In order to be a successful Jew, you must ask yourself the question: "Are your grandchildren Jewish?" and be able to answer in the affirmative. When Ron legally adopted Elisa shortly after our marriage, even the adoption papers stipulated that Elisa would be raised Jewish.

> **...consideration of burial and the afterlife for a Jew are of vital importance.**

In addition, consideration of burial and the afterlife for a Jew are of vital importance. As a Jew, I knew that burial in a Jewish cemetery was a must. We believe that if we are buried in a Jewish cemetery, we will roll underground all the way to Eretz Yisroel and be among the first to be resurrected. As Jews, we believe that we go to Paradise or Abraham's Bosom. If we should accidentally wander to the "other place," Father Abraham "pulls us back."

The importance for me of being an observant Jew is underscored by the following story from the Talmud (Tractate Berachot 28b) about Rabbi Yochanon Ben Zakkai on his deathbed. The rabbi's students were shocked to find their master weeping. Asked to explain his behavior, the sage responded that if he were being taken before a king of flesh and blood whose punishment was *not eternal* and who could be bribed and appeased, he would still be deathly afraid; imagine how he must feel as he finds himself coming before the King of Kings, *who lives forever, whose punishment is eternal and who can neither be bribed nor appeased.* Moreover, two roads lay before him, the sage explained, one led to Heaven and one to hell, and with such prospects, should he not be afraid?

In the January 1989 issue of the *B'nai B'rith Messenger,* "Torah Thoughts," the Rebbe Menachem M. Schneerson writes about this story:

> The Talmud relates that when the great sage Rabbi Yochanon Ben Zakkai wept before his death, he said: 'There are two paths stretching before me, one to Gan Eden [heaven] and one to Gehinom; I know not on which I shall be led.' It goes without saying that Rabbi Yochanon Ben Zakkai was concerned with his spiritual status and if he had attained a sufficient level of holiness to enter heaven.

These concerns are from a man who is credited with the survival of Diaspora Judaism and whose influence has been felt throughout the ages. Rabbi Yochanon Ben Zakkai leaves behind him the expansion of Jewish thought and law, Babylonian Talmud, Responsa literature, Rishonim, Achronim, Chassidut, and Mussar. *But he didn't know for sure whether he was going to Heaven or hell.*

Is it any wonder this story got my attention? If such an eminent and renowned Torah scholar as Rabbi Yochanon Ben Zakkai is uncertain where he is bound, it is incumbent upon us to do whatever is necessary to ensure our future fate and to be deemed worthy of Gan Eden.

Another important consideration regarding Ron's conversion had to do with the Israeli Rabbinate who accept only Orthodox conversions. So we knew that only a kosher conversion would do.

As part of any Jewish conversion, the study of Jewish life, history, and ethics is vital. Ron was exposed to *Yiddishkeit* (Jewish lifestyle) in our home. I looked forward to his education with Rabbi Duchman.

> **As part of any Jewish conversion, the study of Jewish life, history, and ethics is vital.**

Before this conversion was to take place, I wanted to make Ron aware of the three ceremonies that would be required. I explained that males needed to be circumcised, and that since he was already circumcised, the rabbi would draw a bit of blood from the penis as a symbolic gesture. It would also be necessary for him to be immersed in water in a *mikvah*. This is similar to baptism and symbolizes purification and identification with the Jewish people. The third ceremony, though not always done in Reformed or Conservative conversions, must always accompany an Orthodox or "kosher" conversion, and that is the renouncing of a person's prior beliefs before a *Beit Din* or rabbinical court (council of rabbis).

It's So Pagan!

Ron agreed to all the ceremonies but the last one. He said he just didn't think he could renounce Jesus.

I was horrified!

My husband had never mentioned Jesus, hadn't been to church for more than 30 years, and had never used the words "Christian," "Christ," or "New Testament." Here we were leading a Jewish life—we helped to build the synagogue, our home was used by the Jewish community, our daughter was attending Hebrew Academy—*and my husband was telling me he couldn't renounce Jesus!*

> **Ron agreed to all the ceremonies but the last one. He said he just didn't think he could renounce Jesus.**

I was so upset. I said to my husband, "This is crazy. You're such a smart and logical person and such a successful businessman. How can you believe in something so pagan? It's a fantasy. It's like Greek mythology!"

And then in the midst of my horror came this calming thought—I'll just begin to read the Jewish Bible, and in no time at all I will be able to show my husband the Scriptures that will prove to him that Jesus could never have been the fulfillment of the Jewish Bible. I knew that everything God wanted His Jewish people to know about His Jewish Messiah, so that we Jews would recognize Him when He would come, would be in my Jewish Bible.

Is Jesus in the Jewish Bible?

I marched downstairs to the family room and took my Jewish Bible off the shelf. As I opened it that day, I prayed a very specific prayer. I prayed to the God of Abraham, Isaac, and Jacob to show me the truth and to help my husband become a Jew.

That morning as my husband went to work and my daughter to school, I began to read my Bible. I started at page one, "In the beginning," and continued to read page after page. When my husband came home from work and my daughter from school, there I was still reading. The next morning, when my husband went to work and my daughter to school, there I was reading. When they came home again, there I was still reading. This went on for days, for weeks, and then months. I was amazed at what I found written within the pages of my Jewish Bible.

> **I was amazed at what I found written within the pages of my Jewish Bible.**

You see, every Jew feels that he basically knows what's in his own Jewish Bible. That's because as children we attend

Hebrew School, Yeshiva, or Cheder; then as adults, we attend synagogue where we hear a portion read from the Torah and a portion from the *Haftorah* (the Prophets).

Within the pages of my Jewish Bible, there is much written concerning the Messiah—where He would be born, how He would live His life, the miracles He would do. The Bible also speaks of His suffering and death. It frightened me because what I read sounded very much like what I heard said about Jesus. Whoever may be wondering if Yeshua (Jesus) appears in the Jewish Bible need only read the many passages concerning the *Malach Ha Shem*, The Messenger of the Lord. By carefully studying the passages concerning His appearances and how He conducts Himself, one can only deduce that this is no mere created being. He speaks as God and accepts the worship that can *only* be given to God Himself. And He carries in Him the ineffable name of God, the Tetragrammaton, in Hebrew, the *Yud Hay Vav Hay* (see Exod. 23:21).

In addition, *Yeshua*, Jesus' Hebrew name, means "salvation." Everywhere in the Jewish Bible and our Jewish Holy Prayer books, whenever the word "salvation" appears, we are saying Jesus' Hebrew name, Yeshua.

In Proverbs 30:4 I found that God has a Son...

In Isaiah 49:6, the Scriptures speak of a time when the Suffering Servant would lament to God of how He had failed to restore the 12 tribes of Israel. God responds by saying, "It's too light a thing for You to be a servant for Israel only, I will give You as a light to all the nations of the world." In Hebrew the word translated "nations" is *goyim*. So I had to ask myself the question, When did the Messiah come and fail to bring back the tribes of Israel, and then when did God give the Messiah to the goyim?

God Had a Son?

I learned that the ancient Jewish writers recognized that there are two pictures of the Messiah depicted in the pages of the Jewish Bible. They even had names for them: *Moshiach Ben Yoseph* (Messiah, son of Joseph)—the suffering servant Messiah, and *Moshiach Ben Dovid* (Messiah, son of David)—the Messiah who would come as the conquering hero.

In Proverbs 30:4 I found that God has a Son:

> *Who was it that ascended into heaven, and came down again? who gathered the wind in his fists? who bound the waters in a garment? who set up all the ends of the earth? what is his name, and what is his son's name, if thou knowest it?*

Could the Rebbe Be the Messiah?

When I finished reading all the pages of my Jewish Bible, I was confused and frightened. The thought came to me, *Sharon, how dare you think that you could interpret the Bible by yourself, as if you knew as much as a rabbi.* But then I would think about the passages I read where God told the children of Israel to come and hear His Word for themselves (see Deut. 4:10,29; 11:18-20; and Jer. 29:13).

I knew I couldn't stop there. There was too much at stake.

How could I even bear the thought of being an outcast from my people? How absurd it was to think that a man the Gentiles call Jesus Christ could be a Messiah for the Jews. So I said to myself, "Sharon, you must have missed something!"

I remembered that the rabbis say, "You cannot understand the Bible without the Jewish Commentaries." So I bought the Rashi commentaries, the Soncino commentaries, and the latest Jewish commentaries called *The ArtScroll Tanach Series* by Mesorah Publications. And as I read the commentaries, the more I wanted to read. I also brought home texts from the *Babylonian Talmud*, the *Encyclopedia Judaica, Midrash Rabbah, Mishneh Torah* by Maimonides, *Targum Onkelos, Targumim Jonathan, The Messiah Texts* by Raphael Patai, and the *Guide to the Perplexed* by Maimonides. On and on I studied, day after day. With each text I studied, I thought maybe this one will hold the answer, the key to destroying the thought that this *goyishe* messiah is the "real thing"—*the Jewish Messiah!*

All this was beginning to affect my life. When asked if I would accept a role in the leadership as next president of Chabad Women, I felt I had to decline because I was leading a double existence.

I was fully accepted by Chabad and adhered to all the traditions. I even went to a cable television station periodically to hear the Rebbe Menachem M. Schneerson speak to his followers via satellite. I held this man in high esteem. He was respected and consulted by leaders of the world. All of us who listened to him believed that he spoke the truth. It always seemed in those days it could very well be true that one day it would be revealed that the Rebbe Menachem M. Schneerson was the Messiah. It is a popular belief among Chabad followers that in each generation the Messiah dwells among us, but if we are not worthy, he will not be revealed to us. So here I was listening to this Jewish leader believing that he spoke the truth, and yet, at the same time, I was researching ancient Jewish material to find the truth about Jesus! During the next few months, my home library increased. And my fears multiplied proportionately to the number of books I accumulated.

Not to Worry

One afternoon Elisa came home from Hebrew Academy to tell me that they needed mothers to drive students to visit a kosher bakery. She asked if I could volunteer. I was glad to help. That day, while walking through the Fairfax area, I noticed that in the window of the Chabad bookstore there were some anti-missionary books on display. When no one was looking, I dashed back to the bookstore and bought every anti-missionary book available.

I was becoming more and more disturbed by my research. To this point I had studied in private. Only my family knew what I was reading. But the time had come for outside help, and so I turned to my rabbi. I called Mendel and Rochel and asked them to come to my home. When they arrived, we sat in the library, and I showed them my books. I told them that when I read my Bible, I saw Jesus. I asked Mendel to help me. They whispered to each other. Then they turned to me, and Mendel said, "Not to worry." He had just the man for me—a professional who works with people like myself. He would give him my phone number, and the man would call me. I thanked them as they left. I felt so grateful and relieved that I was going to get the help I needed and the answers I so desperately wanted.

> **I told them that when I
> read my Bible, I saw Jesus.**

Two nights later I received a phone call from Rabbi Ben Tzion Kravitz. I gave him a little background about my research and explained how it began. He listened and told me not to worry. He even mentioned a videotape he possessed of people who had renounced their faith in Jesus. I told him to bring it with him when he came to my house.

It was a lovely, sunny, clear morning when Rabbi Kravitz came to my house. I had prepared fresh fruit on a paper plate for the rabbi. I wanted him to know that I was familiar with the Laws of Kashrut, but would honor his hesitancy to eat anything away from his home. I did not wish to cause him any concern about what he was served.

When the rabbi arrived, I introduced him to Ron, who then retired to the upstairs where he spent the day working. Ron remained at home, not because I feared the rabbi, but because it was not appropriate for the rabbi and me to be alone.

For the next ten hours, the rabbi and I discussed the Bible, Jewish history, and tradition. The rabbi had a very modern approach to the Scriptures, and I, a very traditional one. After reading the Talmud, Midrash, Targumim, and other commentaries, I wanted to talk about what our forefathers believed and what the ancient Jewish writings had to say concerning the Messiah.

Desperately Seeking the Truth

After many conversations, the rabbi suggested I talk to someone else. He recommended Gerald Sigal in Brooklyn, New York, author of *The Jew and the Christian Missionary*. Rabbi Kravitz said he would call Mr. Sigal, tell him my situation, and let the two of us discuss various issues over the phone.

The rabbi and Mr. Sigal devised a plan. Mr. Sigal would call collect every Monday night. We would discuss various topics, and then he would pose a question that I would research during the week. The following Monday I would give him the answer.

For example, one week Mr. Sigal said that the genealogy of Jesus was faulty because, in Judaism, no women were ever included in the Jewish genealogies. I was puzzled by this statement for I had recently read the long list of genealogies in First Chronicles in Historical Records of the Jewish Bible, and women are mentioned in those records. The women's names were included to further the specific knowledge needed where a father had only daughters and no sons, or when there was more than one wife or there were concubines.

Our conversations continued for some time until Mr. Sigal told Rabbi Kravitz I was "too far gone" to be helped. Rabbi Kravitz was upset with me and said I should have accepted whatever Mr. Sigal said. He accused me of not really wanting to know the truth. The rabbi didn't understand I was desperately seeking the truth and would go to any lengths to find it. Rabbi Kravitz was probably embarrassed too because Rabbi Duchman kept asking him, "Haven't you helped her yet?"

When I Read My Bible I See "That Man"!

A short time after this, I received a phone call from Rabbi Duchman. He told me about an internationally known deprogrammer, Rabbi J. Immanuel Schochet, who would be speaking soon at my daughter's Yeshiva. I said I would attend.

The night I heard Rabbi Schochet proved to be a turning point in my search for the truth. My family and I sat up front because my daughter was attending the academy, and we felt comfortable sitting close to the speaker.

Earlier that evening Ron, Elisa, and I had decided that we would just go to listen, and we wouldn't say anything until the entire program was over. Then, and only then, would I quietly go up to the rabbi and ask him if he could help me.

The rabbi's speech centered on the generalities of Jewish home life and the problems facing the family. He also discussed various religions and how they differed from Judaism.

After the rabbi completed his talk, he asked for questions. One person asked the rabbi what he could do to protect his children from Christian influence. The rabbi stated that if traditions were respected and followed within a Jewish home, there would be less of a chance for a child to go astray.

Another person expressed his concern about missionaries who wanted to teach his children about Jesus. The rabbi reiterated the value of having Jewish traditions in the home, but also stressed the importance of sending our children to Jewish day schools and Yeshivas.

The third question came from a man who asked what he should do when his child comes home asking him about Scriptures with which he as a Jewish parent is not familiar.

At this point, Rabbi Schochet grabbed the sides of the podium and shouted to the audience, "Never under any circumstances does a knowledgeable Jew ever turn to That Man!" ("That Man" is a name that Jews call Jesus when they don't want to say His name.)

I felt the rabbi was talking directly to me, so I grabbed Ron's hand and whispered, "Should I say something?!"

And Ron said, "Yes!"

I then grabbed Elisa's hand and whispered, "Should I say something?!"

And Elisa said, "Yes!"

So I raised my hand and asked, "Rabbi, what do you tell someone like me who knows Yiddishkeit, follows Judaism, has a Jewish home, and yet, when I read the Jewish Bible, I see *That Man!!?*"

With so many Jewish families and rabbis in the room, my question hit like a bombshell. For the next four or five hours until midnight, Rabbi Schochet and I discussed Yiddishkeit, Jewish customs, the Bible, and other subjects. When midnight approached, the rabbi was anxious to close the meeting, so he said what he considered to be the words that would show me and all the others in the room why Jesus could not be the promised Messiah. He shouted to the audience that Jesus committed blasphemy from the cross.

Then in an angry, mocking tone, the rabbi quoted Jesus saying, "My God, My God, Why hast Thou forsaken Me?"

I was horrified at Rabbi Schochet's tone of voice and accusation that Jesus had committed blasphemy. I told him there were many ways that Jesus could have made that statement. He could have cried out in a plaintive voice or in a pleading or beseeching voice. But Rabbi Schochet refused to see my point of view. I found it amazing that in his anger, he apparently forgot that the statement Jesus made on the cross was first said by our own beloved King David in Psalm 22. *And would any Jew dare to say that David committed blasphemy?!*

> **That night I told my husband and daughter, "I have no more doubts... Jesus is my Jewish Messiah."**

I do not profess to be a Hebrew scholar or a Bible scholar. I am only a plain, ordinary Jewish woman who loves Yiddishkeit and who just wanted to know the truth.

That night I told my husband and daughter, "I have no more doubts...Jesus is my Jewish Messiah."

Commentary by Sid Roth

There are three major reasons some Jewish people don't investigate the claims of Jesus as Messiah. First, the most anti-Semitic people, historically, have called themselves Christians. By definition, the name "Christian" means a follower of the Messiah. Any person who is prejudiced and violent is the farthest thing from being a follower of the Messiah. These "Christians" may have worn large crosses and attended church, but their actions proved they were not followers of the Messiah, the Prince of Peace.

Second, we Jews believe in One God. Believers in the Messiah also believe in One God. But God's essence is infinite, beyond complete comprehension. The rabbis even called Him the *Eyn Sof*—the One Without End. From the Scriptures, we understand our One God can manifest Himself in more than one way. There is much evidence of this in the Torah. Did you ever wonder who was with God when He made man?—"Let *Us* make man in *Our* image, after *Our* likeness..." (Gen. 1:26).

My favorite passage that illustrates this unique nature is Genesis 19:24: "And the *Lord* rained upon Sodom and upon Gomorrah brimstone and fire, from the *Lord,* out of heaven." How could the Lord be in Heaven and also on earth simultaneously? Why must the One true God be as limited as man?

Incidentally, I don't pray to the Messiah; *I pray to God in the Name of the Messiah.* My forefathers prayed to God through the Jewish high priest. My High Priest is Jesus.

The last reason some Jewish people don't seek after Jesus is because the rabbis tell them if they believe in Jesus, they will no longer be Jewish. But if Jesus is the Jewish Messiah, then *there is nothing more Jewish than believing in Him.* So the question is not, How can you be Jewish and believe in Jesus? but rather, Who is Jesus?

The followers of Rabbi Schneerson that Sharon mentioned could have saved themselves a lot of trouble if they had thought for themselves. The Messiah had to be born in Bethlehem according to our Scriptures. Rabbi Schneerson never even *visited* Israel!

In fact, all rabbis worldwide could save themselves a lot of trouble if they understood why Rabbi Yochanon Ben Zakkai, the architect of modern-day rabbinic Judaism, didn't know whether he personally would go to Heaven or hell. A famous rabbi said, "If a blind man follows another blind man, won't both fall into a ditch?"

Is there life after death? With all the books about people who have died or had near-death experiences and gone to Heaven or hell, there can be little doubt. But what do our Jewish Scriptures tell us about life after death?

Daniel 12:1-2 says,

> *At that time shall thy people be delivered, every one that shall be found written in the book [of life]. And many of those that sleep in the dust of the earth shall awake, some to everlasting life, and some to disgrace and everlasting abhorrence.*

Only those whose names are recorded in the book of life go to everlasting life in Heaven. Is your name in the book of life? If you don't know for sure before you die, your fate is everlasting abhorrence (hell). The only way to know for sure is to know God. Not know about Him. Not just believe in Him. You must *know* Him. You must think for yourself.

CHAPTER 6
BY SID ROTH

CHAPTER 6

There Must Be Something More!

"**B**ecause I work, eat, sleep, and that's the way it goes. There must be something more." These are the words of a song that I wrote shortly after graduating from college.

It seems as though I blinked my eyes, and I was married. I blinked my eyes again, and I had a daughter. I blinked my eyes again, and I had a job as a stockbroker with the largest brokerage firm in the world, Merrill Lynch. But there was something missing. Deep inside I felt a yearning—there had to be something more!

I didn't find it in religion. Both of my parents were Jewish. I attended an Orthodox synagogue and was bar mitzvahed. I was proud of being a Jew. But I found the religion boring and many of the religious people hypocritical. God was just not relevant in my life.

I was proud of being a Jew. But I found the religion boring and many of the religious people hypocritical.

So I looked to money for happiness. My goal was to become a millionaire by age 30. But I blinked my eyes again, and I was 29 with no hope of being a millionaire by 30.

I left my wife, my daughter, my job, and went searching for something more. I had been married young. Perhaps the single life would give me satisfaction. After one year, I knew this was not my answer. Then I took a New Age meditation course. The instructor taught me how to lower my brain waves. When I was in this passive, hypnotic state, I was told to invite a "counselor" into my head. He said this counselor would answer my questions.

On the last day of the course, the instructor tested my new power by giving me the name of a woman I didn't know. Then he asked what was physically wrong with her. I asked my counselor, and he showed me that this woman had cancer of the breast. "Could she have cancer of the breast?" I asked. My answer was correct. I knew it was not a lucky guess.

The power started growing. One day I had the thought, *I would like to open my own investment business.* Almost immediately, a businessman whom I barely knew offered me a free office, secretary, and telephone.

> **"Sid, did you know your
> own Jewish Bible condemns
> your involvement in the occult?"**

Soon after I took advantage of his offer, he asked, "Sid, did you know your own Jewish Bible condemns your involvement in the occult?" He showed me from the Torah, Deuteronomy 18:10-12:

> *There shall not be found among thee any one who causeth his son or his daughter to pass through the fire [child sacrifice], one who useth divination [fortune telling], one who is an observer of times [astrology], or an enchanter [sorcery or omens], or a conjurer [hypnotist, witch]. Or a charmer [casts a magic spell], or a consulter with familiar spirits [medium or someone using channeling or ouija boards], or a wizard [spiritist, Transcendental Meditation, Silva Mind Control, Edgar Cayce], or who inquireth of the dead [channeling, seances, etc.]. For an abomination unto the Lord are all that do these things....*

This businessman told me that the "counselor" who gave me information was a demon and very evil.

The Bible, the Supernatural, and the Jews

Then I read a book by McCandlish Phillips called *The Bible, the Supernatural, and the Jews.*[1] Phillips said that because a Jew is under a covenant with God, he faces an even worse judgment for participating in New Age practices. The book included stories of famous Jewish people who had dabbled in the New Age—and lost their lives.

I decided I had better find out if the Bible really was from God. So I stopped consulting my counselor and started reading the Bible. I soon got the scare of my life. My counselor started cursing me. I realized this counselor had a mind of its own and was from the pit of hell. I *had* to get rid of it. But there was no one I could go to for help.

Then things got worse. I broke into astral projection. This is when your spirit leaves your body. I was afraid my spirit would be unable to find its way back and that my body would be buried alive.

As a young boy I had a great fear of death because I thought that dying meant I would cease to exist. Now death looked like my only way to find relief from this horrible situation.

The Worst Night of My Life

On the worst night of my life, I called my wife and asked her to pray. Then I prayed a prayer of my own: "Jesus, help!" I didn't know if He was real, but I had nowhere else to turn. When I went to bed, I didn't want to wake up. Life was too hard.

The next morning I knew immediately something was different. The evil that had been inside of me was gone. I knew it had to do with that prayer. Suddenly I realized I had no fear. Instead, I felt surrounded by liquid love. Finally I had experienced what the New Age could never give me—the tangible presence of God. I had never felt such peace. And I was convinced that Jesus was my Messiah.

Next I heard the audible voice of God. He told me to return to my wife and daughter. My wife, Joy, had become an agnostic when she was exposed to atheistic professors in college. But when I showed her the predictions about the Jewish people written thousands of years in advance in the Bible, she said, "I must believe the Bible is from God." (See Chapter 10 for further discussion about these predictions.) She became a believer in Jesus shortly thereafter.

Something Wrong With the Rabbi

My mother, a great peacemaker, convinced my father that my newfound belief in Jesus was a phase and it too would pass. I was very concerned for my parents to know the Messiah, and I tried to witness at every opportunity. My mother would listen, but my father would get angry and close his ears. Over the years my parents watched how my marriage was restored. They observed the new stability in my life. They could see I was becoming a real *mensch* (Hebrew word that, roughly translated, means "a good human"). They watched my wife, daughter, sister, brother-in-law, and nephews become believers. When my sister lost her daughter, Cheryl Ann, my parents observed her inner strength in dealing with this tragedy—a strength she had not had previously.

> **My mother, a great peacemaker, convinced my father that my newfound belief in Jesus was a phase and it too would pass.**

One day, after much prayer, my father let me read to him the 53rd chapter of Isaiah. By the time I finished, he was angry and accused me of reading from a Christian Bible because he said I was reading about Jesus. I showed him it was published by the Hebrew Publishing Company, but that was not good enough. He said he would only accept a Bible from his Orthodox rabbi. *Hmm,* I thought, *My father thinks Isaiah is speaking of Jesus.*

So the next day I called our family rabbi for an appointment. When I entered his office, he greeted me with a warm welcome and asked what he could do for me. I asked if he would give me a Bible and inscribe something personal to me. He gladly complied, writing some kind words to me on the inside cover.

I thanked him and left quickly. I could not wait to show this powerful gift to my father. When I arrived, I confidently displayed the inscription to my dad and made sure he read it. Then I began to read the same passage from Isaiah. Now he had only two choices. Either he had to agree Jesus was the Messiah, or he had to think something was wrong with the rabbi. To my shock, he said, "I've always thought there was something wrong with that rabbi." And then he proceeded to tell me how he once saw the rabbi eating out in a restaurant on Yom Kippur—the day of fasting.

Think for Yourself

One afternoon when I went over to my parents' house for a visit, my father was at the racetrack. I decided this was the time to prove to my mother that Jesus was the Messiah. I knew that she had very little knowledge of the Scriptures, did not know if they were true, and gave no thought to an afterlife, although she came from a religious family and attended an Orthodox synagogue.

> **"Mom, did you know the entire history of the Jewish people—past, present, and future—is in the Bible?...**

I started by trying to prove that there is a God and the Bible is His book: "Mom, did you know the entire history of the Jewish people—past, present, and future—is in the Bible? Hundreds of precise predictions have come true already. And the scientific dating of the Dead Sea Scrolls in Israel proves no one entered these predictions in the Bible after the event occurred.

"For instance, God said He would bless us beyond any people that ever lived, if we would be obedient to His laws (see Deut. 28:1). However, if we disobeyed, we would lose

our country, be persecuted and scattered to the four corners of the earth (see Deut. 28:36-37; Isa. 11:12). And wherever we would flee, we would be persecuted (see Deut.
28:65). And, even though many of us would suffer and die,
we would always be preserved as a distinct people (see Jer.
31:36). With the suffering we have gone through as Jews,
you would think every Jew left alive would have assimilated
as a means of self preservation. But against impossible
odds, God has preserved us as a distinct people.

"Then, in the last days a miracle would happen. Israel
would become a Jewish nation (see Jer. 16:15). If there
were no Israel and the UN had to vote on it becoming a
Jewish homeland today, what would the probability be?
Zero would be too generous. That is how impossible it was
in 1948. But God caused a great sign to occur that was of
far greater magnitude than the crossing of the Red Sea as
though it were dry land (see Jer. 16:14-15). And a nation,
Israel, was formed in a day as Isaiah predicted (see Isa.
66:8).

"Amos said once we returned we would *rebuild* the waste
cities (see Amos 9:14). And, if you investigate the history of
Israel, you will find one city is built upon another. Tel Aviv
is as modern and cosmopolitan as any city in the world.
Isaiah even said the desert would blossom as the rose (see
Isa. 35:1). By the way, did you know Israel exports more
roses to Europe than any other nation? Ezekiel prophesied
the reforestation of Israel (see Ezek. 36:8). And Isaiah 35:7
tells us, 'The burning sand will become a pool, the thirsty
ground bubbling springs.' How did Isaiah know 2,700 years

ago that Israel would develop technology that would cause underground water to bubble to the surface supporting the growth of vegetation in the barren desert? Since this water originates from deep within the earth, it comes out warm, allowing growth in any weather![2]

"The only way Isaiah or any of the other prophets could have known these things is if God told them. Two hundred years before Cyrus was born, Isaiah identifies him by name and says God would use this Gentile to build the Jewish Temple and restore the cities in Israel (see Isa. 44:28; 45:1,13). How did Isaiah know his name? And better still, how did God get a heathen to want to restore Jerusalem? Jeremiah prophesied that Israel would go into captivity in Babylon for exactly 70 years (see Jer. 29:10). Guess how many years we were captive in Babylon?

"I could go on and on about the amazing predictions of the Bible that were written thousands of years before the fact, but would you like to know about our future? Since God has demonstrated 100 percent accuracy so far, it is reasonable to expect Him to know our future."

> **...for the first time in her life, she was confronted with the accuracy of God's Word.**

As I quickly moved from Scripture to Scripture, I could tell my mother was impressed with my knowledge of the

Bible. And for the first time in her life, she was confronted with the accuracy of God's Word.

"Mom, Zechariah says that in the last days the whole world will not know what to do with Jerusalem (see Zech. 12:3). Today, the problems of Jerusalem and the tiny nation of Israel are in the news continuously. And Israel will be invaded by many nations. The invading powers are mentioned by name (see Ezek. 38:3-9). It will be a real blood bath; two-thirds of our people will perish (see Zech. 13:8). And when there is no hope left, the Messiah will fight for Israel. Let me read it to you from Zechariah:

> *Then the Lord will go out and fight against those nations, as He fights in the day of battle ... "They [the Jewish people] will look on Me, the one they have pierced, and they will mourn for Him as one mourns for an only child, and grieve bitterly for Him as one grieves for a firstborn son. On that day the weeping in Jerusalem will be great ..."*
> (Zechariah 14:3; 12:10-11).

"Mom, do you know why we will be weeping?" I think this was the first time I paused for air and gave her a chance to speak.

"I guess because we will be so grateful for being spared," she said.

"That is partially right. But the main reason is that we will realize, for the first time, that Jesus is our Messiah, and we missed Him."

"But if Jesus is the Messiah, why don't all the rabbis believe? Sidney, I love you, but you still don't know as much as the rabbis who have studied all their life."

"Mom, the Talmud tells us that years ago, when the rabbis pondered how to recognize the Messiah, they concluded that there would be *two* Messiahs. One would suffer for the people and be like Joseph. He would be rejected by his own people. He is described in Isaiah 53:

> *He was despised and rejected by men, a man of sorrows, and familiar with suffering. Like one from whom men hide their faces He was despised, and we esteemed Him not* (Isaiah 53:3).

"And, according to Daniel 9:26, He would die before the second Temple was destroyed:

> *After the sixty-two 'sevens,' the Anointed One [the Messiah] will be cut off and will have nothing. The people of the ruler who will come will destroy the city and the sanctuary.*

"He would die by crucifixion. David describes this hundreds of years before the first recorded crucifixion. David even saw the guards gambling for his clothes. And he noted that His bones would not be broken because this is the requirement for acceptable sacrifices.

> *I am poured out like water, and all My bones are out of joint. My heart has turned to wax; it has melted away within Me. My strength is dried up like a potsherd, and My tongue sticks to the roof of My mouth; you lay Me in the dust of death…. They have pierced My hands and My feet. I can count all My bones; people stare and gloat over me. They divide My garments among them and cast lots for My clothing* (Psalm 22:14-18).

"He did not die for His own sins but for *our sins*:

> *...we considered Him stricken by God, smitten by Him, and afflicted. But He was pierced for our transgressions, He was crushed for our iniquities; the punishment that brought us peace was upon Him, and by His wounds we are healed* (Isaiah 53:4-5).

"Incidentally, the prophets go on to say His ancestry would be from the line of David (see 2 Sam. 7:12-13); the Gentiles would follow Him (see Isa. 11:10); and He would be born in Bethlehem of Judah (see Micah 5:2). Did you know his mother was living in the wrong place until shortly before His birth? Mary had to go to Bethlehem for a special census for tax purposes at the precise moment of his birth!"

"OK already, so why don't the rabbis see this?" she asked.

"Well, they saw this suffering servant Messiah and called Him 'Messiah ben (son of) Joseph.' But then they found just as many predictions about the Messiah reigning as King and ushering in an age of peace. They called Him 'Messiah ben David,' like King David. How did they reconcile these supposedly contradictory roles? Their theory was that there were two distinct Messiahs. But today it is clear that it is *one* Messiah with *two* appearances. First, he came to initiate the New Covenant prophesied by Jeremiah, to change us from the inside out.

"OK already, so why don't the rabbis see this?" she asked.

*"The time is coming," declares the Lord, "when
I will make a new covenant with the house of
Israel ... and will remember their sins no more"*
(Jeremiah 31:31,34).

"Since we humans are so unclean compared to the holiness of God, we always needed a mediator and the blood of an innocent animal to atone for our sins. During Temple days our intermediary was a high priest. Today our intermediary cleanses us from all sins, the Lamb of God who takes away the sins of the whole world. Then, when we are clean, He actually takes up residence inside our body, which becomes His temple.

"Speaking of two appearances of the Messiah, did you know the first time Moses identified himself as our deliverer we rejected him? (See Exodus 2:11-14.) And the first time Joseph identified himself as our deliverer, his own brothers wanted to kill him (see Gen. 37:8,19-20). Jesus fits this same pattern. His second appearance will be when He comes to rule the world and to usher in an age of peace.

*They will neither harm nor destroy on all My
holy mountain, for the earth will be full of the
knowledge of the Lord as the waters cover the sea*
(Isaiah 11:9).

"Today the rabbis teach us about His second coming, but never mention Messiah Ben Joseph. I found out why when I participated in a debate with a rabbi at the University of Maryland. After the debate, I engaged a young Orthodox rabbinical student in dialogue. I asked him to tell me who Isaiah was speaking of in the 53rd chapter. He amazed me with his answer. He said, 'I can't tell you.'

"'Why?' I quickly asked. 'You know Hebrew better than I. Read it from your *Tanakh* (Old Covenant).'"

"'No,' he responded, 'it would be a sin.'"

"'Why?' I asked again."

"'Because I am not holy enough,' he said. 'We can only tell you what the rabbis who lived closer to the days of Moses tell us the verse means.'"

"How sad, Mom. What he was really saying was *he could not think for himself.*"

Although I thought my presentation to my mother was overwhelming, she let me know she was grateful for the change believing in Jesus had caused in my life, but was not ready to accept the truth. "What would your father say? Are you hungry? Can I get you something to eat?"

> **Over the years, whenever my mother was sick, I would pray for her, and God would heal her. ...Before she died, she too accepted *Yeshua* (Hebrew for Jesus) as her Messiah.**

Over the years, whenever my mother was sick, I would pray for her, and God would heal her. As a Jewish nonbeliever, my mom was so proud of me she would tell all her Jewish friends that if they were sick her son would pray in

Jesus' Name, and God would heal them. Before she died, she too accepted *Yeshua* (Hebrew for Jesus) as her Messiah.

Who Is a True Jew?

But my dad was still embarrassed and very hurt by my faith. He was born in Poland and saw anti-Semitism by so-called "Christians" firsthand. After my mother's funeral, my father had only one question: Was I going to say the prayers (*Kaddish*) for my mother in the synagogue every day for eleven months? There was an ulterior motive behind my father's question. If I would say the prayers for my mother, he could be assured that I would say them for him. And it was his belief that somehow these prayers would be his ticket into Heaven without punishment or delay. Since he knew I did not agree with this form of prayer, he wondered what my answer would be. For a split second I thought of the time commitment. I thought of the endurance needed to sit through all the rituals and prayers in a language I did not understand. I thought of the possible repercussions by those in the synagogue who knew of my outspoken faith in Jesus. But as quickly as these thoughts raced through my mind, I found myself agreeing to do it.

It had been years since I had put on the *tefillin* (little box with Scripture inside that is wrapped around one's head and arm to conform to Deuteronomy 6:8). A retired rabbi helped me as I placed the tefillin around my arm and on my head.

After one service, I got into a conversation with the man who read from the Torah. The Torah reading happened to be about the Jewish people walking through the Red Sea as though it were dry land. As I discussed this with my friend, he looked at me with the most incredulous expression and said, "You don't really believe those stories, do you?"

I responded with just as incredulous an expression and said, "You don't? What are you doing here?"

It is one thing when a secular Jew does not believe in the Torah. But when a Jewish religious leader does not believe, it shocks me. Then, when he told me he did not believe in God or life after death, I was curious why he came to the synagogue at all. He responded, "Because my friends are here. Because I like the traditions of my fathers. And because it gives me something to do."

I always thought these elderly men who *davined* (prayed) every day at the *minyan* (a gathering of ten or more Jewish men to pray) were the most holy Jews in the synagogue. I found that many of the men I prayed with felt the same way as this man.

My father greatly appreciated my going to the synagogue every day to pray. And since I had not mentioned Jesus in a while, he asked, "Do you still believe in Him?" I had been waiting for God's timing because every time I mentioned Jesus, my father would always get angry. I told him that I believed in Jesus and He was the reason I was going to the synagogue. I said I did not believe the prayers were necessary for Mom because she was already in Heaven. At that, he got angry, and I quickly changed the subject.

> **My father would say to me,
> "You're a wonderful son.
> You're as good as gold. But do
> you have to believe in *Him*?"**

On another occasion my father said men from the synagogue had told him that their sons would not have been so faithful to go to the synagogue every day. My father would say to me, "You're a wonderful son. You're as good as gold. But do you have to believe in *Him*?"

The Talmud declares that if a voice from heaven should contradict the majority of rabbis, we must ignore that voice. A *true* Jew says that if the Torah contradicts the majority of the rabbis, we must follow the Torah.

May God grant that soon all Israel would be *true* Jews.

Heaven Must Be a Wonderful Place

Years later, I got a call that my father was dying in the hospital. My sister, also a believer, and I went to his bedside. I felt a strong presence of God that had been on me constantly for several days. It was the same tangible presence as when Jesus first became real to me years earlier. I said, "Dad, do you remember how Mom always said, 'Heaven must be a wonderful place'? Don't you want to be with her and the rest of our family?"

My father had lost his voice. His body was destroyed by cancer. But a great miracle happened. When I asked him if he wanted to make Yeshua his Messiah and Lord, my sister and I heard him say,

"Yes!"

I am a very thankful person. Every member of my immediate Jewish family believes in Yeshua. Joy and I have celebrated 43 years of marriage. My daughter is now married and has three daughters.

> **And I have seen miracles happen thousands of times when I pray for the sick in His name.**

It has been more than 30 years since I was set free. Over time, the mind can play tricks. If this had been my only experience with God, I would begin to doubt. But I have studied the Bible for myself, and I am 100 percent convinced only one person in all of history could be the Jewish Messiah. Daily I experience the presence of God. And I have seen miracles happen thousands of times when I pray for the sick in His name.

Thank God there is something more!

Commentary by Sid Roth

Some people in the New Age believe they have been reincarnated (died and come back as another person or being). Some have testified under hypnosis about experiences in other lives and in countries they have never even visited. How is this possible? The Bible says you die once, and then comes the judgment. This rules out any possibility of reincarnation. Therefore, people who speak of past lives are channeling for familiar spirits. These familiar spirits have been around for thousands of years.

My sister, a sensible, stable elementary school teacher, had also violated Deuteronomy 18 and opened herself up to demonic influence. Years later, she attended a deliverance meeting. As the leader of the meeting prayed for demons to manifest so they could be cast out, she heard some coughs around the room and screaming. The screams got louder. They didn't seem human. My sister hadn't gone to participate, but observe. In her own words:

I was scared and wanted to leave. I turned to tell my husband (a Jewish accountant) that I wanted to go, but I couldn't get an audible word out. My tongue wouldn't lie flat; it kept twisting around in my mouth. Then I looked down at my hands and saw they were both in fists. I couldn't open them. My fingernails dug into my palms. I was paralyzed! The fear was intolerable. I started crying.

Then a man came over to me and said, "Name your demon." I didn't know what he was talking about. Couldn't he see I was paralyzed? When I didn't answer, he walked away. Next a lady came over and said the same thing, "Name your demon." I found the words coming out of my mouth, "Demon of fear." She commanded it to leave. My fists immediately opened up, and I was able to talk. I knew the spirit world was real. That evening I was released from a fear of people that had tormented me my whole life. I was free.

My sister, her husband, and their three sons are now Messianic Jews. I'm glad everyone doesn't have to experience the reality of the dark, invisible world to find the Lord. The devil is real. Demons are real. And the only defense is the Jewish Messiah.

Endnotes

1. McCandlish Philips, *The Bible, the Supernatural, and the Jews* (New York, NY: World Pub. Co., 1970).

2. From an interview with Dr. Dov Pasternack of the Ben Gurion University of the Negev on "Report to Zion," *Messianic Vision* radio broadcast #8 (April 1989).

CHAPTER 7
BY MICHAEL L. BROWN, PH.D.

CHAPTER 7

Tradition or Truth? What I Learned About Rabbinic Judaism

"You don't even know Hebrew! How can you tell me what the Bible says?"

"It's true, Rabbi. I don't know Hebrew—but I *will* learn. In the meantime, I can use the dictionary in the back of Strong's Concordance."

"Meantime, shmeantime. If you don't know Hebrew, it doesn't mean a thing."

I will never forget those words spoken to me in 1972. I was a brand-new believer in Jesus, just 17 years old. My life had been *dramatically* changed—and I mean dramatically. Only months before, I was shooting heroin, using massive quantities of LSD and speed, and living in total, reckless abandon. My nickname, "Drug Bear," was well deserved, and I was sinful, proud, and rotten to the core. All this was in spite of a typical, Long Island, Conservative Jewish upbringing by very happily married parents. In fact, my father was a highly respected lawyer working as the Senior Law Assistant to the New York State Supreme Court judges.

My drug abuse was not due to some inner turmoil or spiritual quest. I used drugs because they made me feel good! You see, I was a fairly talented, teenage rock drummer, and the whole Woodstock, cast-off-restraint, get high, do-your-own-thing mentality appealed to me. I wanted to be like the rock stars! Soon, life became one big party.

The Surprise of My Life

But God had other plans. My two best friends (the bass player and guitar player in our band) were raised in homes that were "Christian" in name only. They were no closer to Jesus than I was. But they were friendly with two girls whose father was a dedicated, "born-again" Christian, and their uncle pastored a little church in Queens, New York. The girls went to the church to please their father, my friends went to the church to spend time with the girls, and then I went to the church to pull them all out. I didn't like the changes I was beginning to see in them!

What happened? I got the surprise of my life. In that little church, I met with the God I was not seeking, and I found out the truth about Jesus, the Savior and Messiah in whom I had never believed. I was transformed! The love of God broke down my resistance, and in answer to the secret prayers of a faithful few, I turned away from the filthy life I had been leading. My father was thrilled to see the change.

He had only one problem: "We're Jewish! Now that you are free from drugs, you need to meet the rabbi and come back to our traditions." And so, I began to talk with the young, scholarly rabbi who had just become the spiritual leader of the synagogue in which I was bar mitzvahed.

I Must Learn Hebrew

I knew beyond any doubt that my experience was real, but how could I answer his questions? What could I say when he told me that the English translation I was using was wrong, and that, time and time again, the New Testament writers misinterpreted the Hebrew Scriptures? He could read the original text. I couldn't! He also brought me to meet with Ultra-Orthodox, Lubavitcher rabbis in Brooklyn who specialized in dealing with "straying" young Jews like me. For my part, I was happy to have the opportunity to share my faith with these sincere men. After all, I was reading the Bible day and night, memorizing hundreds of verses, praying for hours, even persuading a Jewish Jehovah's Witness that her religion was not biblical. But these rabbis in Brooklyn had answers I had never heard before. And all of them had been able to read and understand Hebrew since their childhood. I could barely remember how to pronounce the letters! Plus, they *looked* so Jewish, with long black beards and all. Their faith seemed to be so ancient and authentic. Was mine?

So it was that I began to study Hebrew in college. If my faith was based on truth, it could withstand honest academic scrutiny. If Jesus was really the Jewish Messiah, I had nothing to fear. Serious questions deserved serious answers, and I was determined to follow the truth wherever it led, regardless of the consequences.

> **If Jesus was really the Jewish Messiah, I had nothing to fear. Serious questions deserved serious answers...**

Little by little, I became convinced that I should pursue scholarly biblical and Jewish studies. One year in college I took only language courses, *six* to be exact: Hebrew, Arabic, Greek, Latin, German, and Yiddish. Talk about brain drain! I wanted to read the relevant texts for myself, in the original languages, without anyone's help.

But college was not enough. In order to pursue my goals, graduate school was necessary. There I could study the other ancient languages relevant to the Hebrew Scriptures, languages like Akkadian (that is, Babylonian and Assyrian), Ugaritic (from a major city north of Canaan), Aramaic, Syriac, Phoenician, Punic, Moabite— the list goes on. By the time I wrote my doctoral dissertation, I had studied about 15 languages, some in great depth, others only superficially. I received my Ph.D. from New York University in Near Eastern languages.

Faulty Foundations

Almost all my courses were taught by Jewish professors and, along the way, I also had the opportunity to do some private study with several rabbis. What happened to my faith? It actually became *stronger*. As I learned more, I became even more convinced that Jesus was the prophesied Messiah, the one whose life, atoning death, resurrection, and return were foreshadowed in the Hebrew Scriptures. I had sound answers for serious questions!

I also discovered something unexpected: It was not the New Testament faith that was built on faulty foundations; the foundations of *rabbinic Judaism* were faulty! It was rabbinic Judaism, not the New Testament faith, that deviated from the Hebrew Bible.

> **It was not the New Testament faith that was built on faulty foundations; the foundations of *rabbinic Judaism* were faulty!**

Rabbinic Judaism does not even claim to be based upon a literal interpretation of the Scriptures. Instead, the rabbis say that their faith is the continuation of an unbroken chain of *tradition* dating back to Moses and the prophets. This is a crucial point. As we will see later, such an unbroken chain does not exist.

I have often heard rabbis and anti-missionaries say—in a somewhat derogatory tone—that without Christ there could be no Christianity (or, without Messiah there could be no Messianic Judaism), whereas Judaism can exist without a Messiah, important as such a figure is in Jewish thinking. Judaism, it is claimed, is the religion of the Torah.

Of course, I agree that there could be no Christianity without a Christ, just as I agree that there could be no salvation without a Savior and no deliverance without a Deliverer. This presents no problem at all. Our faith is based on the person and work of the Messiah.

But the real question is the following: on what foundation is traditional Judaism based? Judaism as we know it today is not the religion of the Torah as much as it is *the religion of rabbinic tradition*. Without tradition, there could be no traditional Judaism; without the rabbis, there could be no rabbinic Judaism. This is very significant! For many of our people, human tradition is more important than biblical truth.

More than 20 years ago, an Orthodox rabbi told me I was reading the Scriptures through rose-colored glasses. In other words, I would always misunderstand the Word no matter how sincere I tried to be. I wasn't seeing clearly. My vision was distorted.

> **More than 20 years ago, an Orthodox rabbi told me I was reading the Scriptures through rose-colored glasses.**

That was quite an accusation, and I didn't take it lightly. I studied the Word from every possible angle, asking myself whether other interpretations were correct, challenging the standard Christian answers with which I was familiar. Now, almost a quarter of a century later, I can honestly say that it is religious Jews—in spite of their sincerity and devotion— who read the Bible with colored glasses. They will be the first to tell you that *the Bible says only what the sages tell them it says.*

Who are they to differ with the great Jewish teachers of the past? Who are they to disagree with the famous rabbinic commentaries of the middle ages? How could they possibly break with the traditions they learned from their fathers? "After all, what can I know? My father learned it from his father who learned it from his father, who learned it from his father, and so on, all the way back to Moses. Are you telling me they made it up? Are you telling me they were deceived? How dare you question our sacred traditions!"

And so the myth of an unbroken chain of tradition going back to Moses has kept many Jewish people from reading the Bible on their own. This is the heart of the matter.

The Game of Telephone

Rabbinic Judaism believes that God gave Moses a Written Law (found in the Torah, the five books of Moses). But, we are told, most of the commandments in the Law are briefly worded, general statements, something like the headings of a paragraph in a book. They need interpretation. They need to be expanded and explained. So, according to the traditional belief, God also gave Moses an Oral

Law that interpreted the Written Law. Moses then passed this on to Joshua, who passed it on to the 70 leading elders in his generation, who passed it on to the prophets of the next generations.

And so it went, but not without lots of additions. This is because the rabbis teach that the Oral Law kept growing, since in every generation, new traditions were developed and new situations emerged which called for new applications of the Law.

Within two centuries after the time of Jesus, this Oral Law was so bulky and complex that it had to be written down lest it be forgotten (that's right, the basics of the *Oral* Law were now *written*). This became the Mishnah, which was expanded into what is known as the Talmud over the next few centuries. After that, according to the rabbinic belief, those who studied the Talmud continued to develop and pass down the Oral Law to each succeeding generation. *Every religious Jew believes with all his heart that it is impossible to understand the Scriptures or follow God's Law without these oral traditions.*

And what happens when an observant Jew is approached by a Jewish believer in Jesus? The believer is regarded as an ignorant newcomer, and his interpretations are totally scorned: "We have an unbroken tradition going back to Moses! How dare you differ with us! How dare you try to teach us!" Yes, tradition carries quite a lot of weight. And it can stop people from thinking for themselves. (I find it amusing, to say the least, when Orthodox Jews tell me that *I* have been brainwashed!)

> **What happens when an observant Jew is approached by a Jewish believer in Jesus? The believer is regarded as an ignorant newcomer, and his interpretations are totally scorned...**

Now you can better understand why so many Jews with whom believers try to dialog will immediately say: "I have to ask my rabbi. He will tell me what that verse really means. He will look it up in his books." You see, the rabbinic Jew believes that the further back in time you go, the closer you get to the original revelation at Mount Sinai (kind of like a thirty-five-hundred-year-old game of "telephone"). And Talmudic tradition teaches that, since the days of Moses, we have been on a steady spiritual decline. This is all the more reason that we have to depend on the views of the earlier generations! They were closer to those who received the original revelation, and they were on a higher spiritual plane. *They* can tell us what the Scripture means. Talk about reading the Bible through colored glasses!

Are the Traditions True?

"But," someone might ask, "how can you be so sure that these traditions aren't true? Why do you say that they don't provide the correct interpretations?" The answers are simple: 1) They take for themselves an authority that the Scriptures never gave them. 2) They put the voice of earthly reason on a higher plane than the prophetic word from Heaven. 3) They contradict the plain meaning of the Scriptures. 4) At times they even contradict the voice of God. 5) There is *no* biblical evidence for an unbroken chain of tradition and *plenty* of evidence against it.

Before I give you some examples, I want you to understand that this is not a matter of finding minor contradictions and interpretative difficulties. No. The issues here deal with the very heart and soul of traditional Judaism, a religion which stands or falls on its traditions.

The question that every honest Jew must ask is:

What if the Bible says one thing and my traditions say another? Will I follow God, or will I follow man?

It is not a question of whether these Jewish leaders were evil men and deceivers. Most of them were zealous for their faith. They sought to lead good lives and please the Lord. But were they right? Did their traditions really originate with God, or did they originate with man? Let's take a careful look. None of the examples that follow are taken out of context in any way. They are plain and straightforward.

First, let's see what traditional Judaism says of itself. According to the contemporary Orthodox scholar H. Chaim Schimmel, the Jewish people "*do not follow the literal word of the Bible*, nor have they ever done so. They have been fashioned and ruled by the verbal interpretation of the written word...."[1]

As expressed by Rabbi Z.H. Chajes, a leading 19th-century authority, the Talmud indicates that the words "that were transmitted orally" by God are "more valuable" than those transmitted in writing. Chajes goes so far as to say that

> allegiance to the authority of the said rabbinic tradition is binding upon all sons of Israel…. And he who does not give adherence to the unwritten Law and the rabbinic tradition has no right to share the heritage of Israel….[2]

How can such a claim be made? The rabbis assert that *it is the Bible itself* that gives them the exclusive authority to interpret Torah and develop new laws. They find support for this in Deuteronomy 17:8-12, probably the most important text in the Bible for rabbinic Judaism. This is what the verses say:

> *If cases come before your courts that are too difficult for you to judge—whether bloodshed, lawsuits, or assaults—take them to the place the Lord your God will choose. Go to the priests, who are Levites, and to the judge who is in office at that time. Inquire of them and they will give you the verdict. You must act according to the decisions they give you at the place the Lord will choose. Be careful to do everything they direct you to do. Act according to the law they teach you and the decisions they give you. Do not turn aside from what they tell you, to the right or to the left. The man who shows contempt for the judge or for the priest who stands ministering there to the Lord your*

God must be put to death. You must purge the evil from Israel.

What Moses is clearly saying is that in every generation the Levitical priests and the current "judge" in Jerusalem would function as a kind of Supreme Court, a court of final appeal, the likes of which exist today in many nations around the world, including Israel and the United States. This court would be responsible for settling disputes regarding various legal matters such as homicide, civil law, and assaults. That's it! The text does not give any authority to subsequent generations of rabbis around the world (where does it even mention rabbis?), nor does it give *anyone* authority to tell all Jews when to pray, what to pray, how to slaughter their cattle, what to believe about the Messiah, when to visit the sick, whether or not one can write on the Sabbath, and on and on and on. Nothing of the sort! Yet, it is from this little text that the sages have derived so much power.

As for verse 11, which says, "Act according to the law they teach you and the decisions they give you. *Do not turn aside from what they tell you, to the right or to the left,*" this was actually interpreted by the 13th-century commentator Nachmanides to mean the following: "Even if it seems to you as if they are changing 'right' into 'left'...it is incumbent on you to think what they say is 'right' is 'right.'"[3] Why? Because the Spirit of God is on them, and the Lord will keep them from error and from stumbling. This is quite a claim! If the sages tell you that left is right, you are to follow the sages. Let's take this a step further. What if

1,000 prophets of the caliber of Elijah and Elisha tell you that the Torah means one thing, but 1,001 sages tell you it means something else? Whom do you follow? Maimonides, the most influential medieval Jewish scholar, is emphatic: "The final ruling is in accordance with the 1,001 sages."[4] Yes, the Talmud even teaches that if Elijah himself differed with a rabbinic *tradition* or a prevailing *custom* of the people—not a biblical Law itself but simply a tradition or custom concerning that Law—then he should not be followed.[5]

"But," you might say, "there may be something to that. Shouldn't we follow the plain and obvious meaning of the Bible even if some prophet claims that God told him otherwise?" Of course we should. But that is *not* what Maimonides was saying. He actually argued that if someone like Elijah favored the plain and obvious meaning of the Scriptures instead of the rabbinic tradition, the tradition was to be followed.

So even a proven prophet, backed by the power of God and following the plain sense of the Bible, has less weight than rabbinic tradition. And the sages, by a majority of even one, outweigh the likes of Elijah and Elisha when it comes to interpreting the Law. Are things getting clearer now?

More Weight—Rabbis or God?

But it doesn't stop there: A legal decision made by the majority of the sages *carries more weight than even the voice of God!* According to one of the most famous stories in the Talmud (Baba Mesia 59b), there was a dispute between

Rabbi Eliezer the Great and the sages about whether or not a particular kind of oven was ritually clean. He answered every one of their arguments, but they refused to accept his decision. Rabbi Eliezer then called upon a series of miracles to verify his ruling: If the Law is in accordance with me, then let this carob tree be uprooted; let this stream of water stop flowing; let the walls of this house of study collapse. Amazingly, the Talmud teaches that each miracle happened, but still the other rabbis refused to be moved.

Finally, Rabbi Eliezer called on God Himself to verify his position. Immediately, a voice came from Heaven saying, "Why are you troubling Rabbi Eliezer? The legal ruling is always in accordance with him." To which Rabbi Joshua exclaimed, "It is not in Heaven!" In other words, since the Torah was given at Mount Sinai (and is therefore no longer "in Heaven"), legal decisions are to be made solely on the basis of human reasoning and logical deduction. Period. As expressed by the legal authority Rabbi Aryeh Leib, "Let the truth emerge from the earth. The truth be as the sages decide with the human mind."[6]

And so if God speaks—as He did here—the sages can (and should!) overrule Him if they disagree with His interpretation. What was the basis for such an incredible position? The Talmud cites the last three words of Exodus 23:2 and interprets them to mean, "Follow the majority." But the text says the exact opposite! Just read the whole verse. The meaning is clearly, "*Don't* follow the majority." Even J. H. Hertz, the former chief rabbi of England, wrote, "The Rabbis disregarded the literal meaning of the last three

Hebrew words, and took them to imply that, except when it is 'to do evil,' one should follow the majority."[7]

And that is their support for negating and disregarding the voice of God! A verse that says "Don't follow the majority" was sliced up and reinterpreted so as to mean, "Follow the majority," and, on this basis, God Himself was overruled. It almost takes your breath away.

Can Rabbis Change the Torah?

Amazingly, the Talmudic text goes on to say that Elijah later informed one of the rabbis that God laughed about the incident saying, "My sons have defeated Me!" Talk about "majority rules"! Not only is it true that 1,000 prophets following the plain sense of the Scripture don't stand a chance against 1,001 sages, but God Himself doesn't stand a chance against even two sages should they beg to differ with Him! Did you have any idea that the power of tradition and human authority went so far?

> **Not only is it true that 1,000 prophets following the plain sense of the Scripture don't stand a chance against 1,001 sages, but God Himself doesn't stand a chance against even two sages should they beg to differ with Him!**

It is not that these rabbis were arrogant or irreverent. They simply believed that it was their God-given duty to interpret and make Laws, and, over the process of time, they came to believe that their traditions were sacred. They even claimed to have the right to *change* the biblical Laws if necessary. What was their scriptural support for this? Psalm 119:126: "It is time for you to act, O Lord; Your law is being broken." To which you might say, "I don't get it. What has this verse got to do with changing the Law?" Nothing. But it was totally reinterpreted (actually, totally *mis*interpreted) to mean: "Sometimes, in order to act for the Lord, it is necessary to dissolve His Laws."[8] I kid you not. Is it any wonder, then, that at times the Talmud credits the sages with "uprooting Scripture" with their interpretations?[9] This is something worth remembering the next time someone tries to tell you that Jesus and Paul freely went around breaking and changing the laws.

And where do the rabbis claim that the Bible itself makes reference to the Oral Law? One key text is Exodus 34:27:

> *Then the Lord said to Moses, "Write down these words, for in accordance with these words I have made a covenant with you and with Israel."*

What does this verse have to do with the *Oral* Law? Nothing at all! The context speaks of Laws to be *written down*.

How then did the authors of the Talmud find a reference here to the *unwritten* Law? First, they failed to quote the beginning of the verse ("*Write down* these words"). Then, they noticed that the Hebrew phrase translated "in accordance with" (*'al pî*) was very close to the Hebrew phrase for "oral" (*'al peh*). So, the verse was understood as if it said, "Write down these words, for on the testimony over these words, I have made a covenant with you and with Israel." But that is *not* what the Hebrew says, as any reliable Jewish translation of the Bible will tell you at once. A play on words is one thing; the real meaning is something else.

And how did Rashi, the greatest of all Jewish biblical commentators, handle the clear meaning of this verse that the covenant was based on the *written Word?* He interpreted "Write down these words" to mean *these words only,* explaining that "it is not permitted to write down the words of the Oral Law."[10] So, God says, "Write!" but the tradition says, "Don't write it all!" God makes His covenant with Israel based on what was transmitted in writing; the Talmud says that the real essence of the covenant was based on what was transmitted orally. And isn't it strange that a biblical text clearly emphasizing the *Written Law* was utilized by the Talmud to point to the *Oral Law*—based on a play on words alone? What an example of grasping at straws!

The complete absence of any mention of an Oral Law in the Hebrew Bible stands in direct contrast to the frequent references to the binding nature of the Written Law found throughout the Scriptures. Just read verses like Deuteronomy 31:24-26:

> *After Moses finished writing in a book the words of this law from beginning to end [and notice: there was no part of the Law that Moses failed to write down; he wrote it all, from beginning to end], he gave this command to the Levites who*

> *carried the ark of the covenant of the Lord: "Take*
> *this Book of the Law and place it beside the ark of*
> *the covenant of the Lord your God. There it will*
> *remain as a witness against you."*

There are plenty of other verses that say the same thing, such as Exodus 24:7-8; Deuteronomy 17:14-20; 28:58-59; 30:9-10; Joshua 1:8; 23:6; First Kings 2:1-3; Second Kings 22:13; 23:3,21; First Chronicles 16:39-40; Second Chronicles 30:5; 31:3; 35:26-27; Ezra 3:2-4; 6:18; Nehemiah 10:28-29; 13:1; and Daniel 9:13. I encourage you to look up these verses and read them carefully. Where is there any mention of an Oral Law?[11]

And if there were such an authoritative chain of interpretation, why are there so many disagreements about the Law on virtually every page of the Talmud? One could almost say that the Talmud *consists* of disagreements and discussions about the interpretation and application of the Law. And why do the great rabbinic commentaries differ on the meaning of hundreds and hundreds of biblical verses? Where is the authoritative chain of tradition?

> **And if there were such an authoritative**
> **chain of interpretation, why are there**
> **so many disagreements about the Law**
> **on virtually every page of the Talmud?**

No, God did not give an Oral Law to Moses on Mount Sinai. The very first mention of even the *concept* of such a binding, oral tradition is more than 1,400 years *after* Moses. What's more, many of the Jewish groups that existed in Jesus' day, such as the Sadducees and the Essenes, had no belief in any such tradition. That was a distinct doctrine of the Pharisees. Why? Because they were the ones who invented the whole idea of an unbroken chain of binding, oral tradition, beginning shortly before Jesus came into the world. And, as they passed their unique traditions on to their successors, the new generations began to say: "We didn't invent these teachings, we inherited them. They have been passed on to us from our fathers. They go back many years…way back…as far back as we can remember…all the way back to Moses." Not quite!

Let the truth be told. There was no secret Law given to Moses by word of mouth or passed on by him orally to the biblical prophets and leaders. Actually, our forefathers sometimes forgot the *Written Law* (read Second Kings 22 for a classic example of this). An *Oral Law* wouldn't have stood a chance. And there is not a single example in the Scriptures where anyone was ever punished, rebuked, or held accountable for breaking any so-called binding *tradition*. That's because there was no such tradition to break. Only violations of the written Word were considered sinful.

The Truth

Now it's time to listen to that Word. The Torah tells us that wherever we Jews are, even scattered around the world, "if from there you seek the Lord your God, you will find Him if you look for Him with all your heart and with all your soul" (Deut. 4:29). Jeremiah the prophet gave the same message: "You will seek Me and find Me when you seek Me with all your heart" (Jer. 29:13). And the Book of Proverbs says,

> *Trust in the Lord with all your heart and lean not on your own understanding; in all your ways acknowledge Him, and He will make your paths straight* (Proverbs 3:5-6).

God will not let you down—if you sincerely seek His truth. Why not humble yourself and ask for His help? There is a place for reason and rational discussion, and there is a place for seeking God too. They go hand in hand! But the Lord opposes those who are wise in their own eyes. Study the Word *and* seek God. You will not be disappointed.

When Moses and the prophets couldn't figure out how to interpret or apply the Law, they prayed and asked God for the answer. And God showed them what to do![12] Why not follow their lead? Why be smarter than Moses and the prophets and try to figure it all out for yourself?

**Ask God to guide
you into the truth.**

Study, yes, by all means. But ask God to open your eyes when you do! (That's exactly how the Psalmist prayed in Psalm 119:18.) Ask God to guide you into the truth.

It is not that the rabbis meant evil. They really believed in what they did, and there is often beauty and wisdom in their words. They were totally committed to their traditions, and through these traditions, they sought to bind the people of Israel together. But, while the traditions may have bound us together, they have, more importantly, bound us up. You can be free today.

"To the Jews who had believed Him, Jesus said, 'If you hold to My teaching, you are really My disciples. Then you will know the truth, and the truth will set you free'" (John 8:31-32).

Commentary by Sid Roth

I never heard much talk about the Messiah when I was a child. At our Passover seder we would open the door for Elijah to announce the Messiah. But the adults viewed the event as a fairy tale, almost like the Jewish version of Santa Claus. As I got older, I realized it was just "pretend," but I went along with the charade for the sake of the young children and "tradition."

Every Passover we read Psalm 118:22: "The stone which the builders rejected is become the chief cornerstone." Now I know that the cornerstone we builders (the Jewish people) rejected is the Messiah. No wonder Elijah never came to our Passover seder. Messiah had already come to die at Passover. Isaiah 53:7 says He was "like the [Passover] lamb which is led to the slaughter."

The name "Passover" comes from Exodus 12:13:

> *And the blood shall be to you for a token upon the houses where ye are; and when I see the blood, I*

will pass over you; and there shall be no plague against you to destroy....

But why was blood necessary? Leviticus 17:11 says,

For the life of the flesh is in the blood; and I have appointed it for you upon the altar to make an atonement for your souls; for the blood it is that maketh an atonement for the soul.

In other words, a blood sacrifice was the only acceptable substitute to atone for sin. During the first Passover, the blood was to be applied to the doorposts. Later, under the Mosaic Covenant, an animal had to be sacrificed in the Temple on the altar (see Lev. 1:11).

This is why we read in the Talmud, Yoma 5a, there can be no Yom Kippur without blood. Since the Temple was destroyed in A.D. 70, *there have been no Temple sacrifices for forgiveness of sin.*

In fact, *40 years before* the Temple was destroyed, the ancient rabbis recognized ominous supernatural signs that God no longer accepted the animal sacrifices that were offered (Yoma 39a,b). *That was the year Jesus died for our sins.*

Even the Jewish prophet Daniel said our Messiah would come and die, not for His own sins, but for ours *before* the Temple was destroyed (see Dan. 9:26).

True Judaism requires the blood of atonement of Jesus!

Since we have no Temple today, either our sins cannot be atoned for, or God has already sent His Messiah.

Of whom is this Yom Kippur prayer from a traditional Jewish prayer book speaking?

> Our righteous anointed is departed from us: horror hath seized us, and we have none to justify us. He hath borne the yoke of our iniquities and our transgression, and is wounded because of our transgression. He beareth our sins on His shoulder, that He may find pardon for our iniquities. We shall be healed by His wound, at the time that the Eternal will create Him as a new creature.[13]

Endnotes

1. H. Chaim Schimmel, *The Oral Law: A Study of the Rabbinic Contribution to Torah She-Be-Al-Peh*, rev. ed. (Jerusalem, New York, NY: Feldheim, 1987), italics added.

2. Z.H. Chajes, *The Student's Guide Through the Talmud*, trans. and ed. Jacob Schacter (New York, NY: Feldheim, 1960), 4.

3. See Nachmanides to Deuteronomy 17:11 and also the Babylonian Talmud, Baba Batra 12a.

4. See Maimonides' introduction to his commentary on the Mishnah.

5. See again Maimonides' introduction to his commentary on the Mishnah, and also the Babylonian Talmud, Yebamot 102a.

6. See the introduction to his *Ketzot HaHoshen* on *Hoshen Mishpat* in *Shulhan Arukh*.

7. Dr. J.H. Hertz, *The Pentateuch and Haftorahs* (London: Soncino, 1978), 316. The only real issue is whether to translate the Hebrew word *rabbîm* in this verse with "many" or "mighty." (The Talmudic passage in Baba Mesia 59b, of course, understood the word to mean "many"—in other words, the majority.) Either way, the meaning is impossible to dispute: *don't* follow the *rabbîm*!

8. See the Babylonian Talmud, Berakot 54a.

9. See, for example, the Jerusalem Talmud, Kiddushin 1:2, 59d; the Babylonian Talmud, Sotah 16a, with Rashi's comments to the words 'oqeret and halakah.

10. See also Gittin 60a in the Babylonian Talmud.

11. It is possible that a rabbinic Jew might point to Nehemiah 8:8, the only verse which mentions that the Levites made the Law clear as it was being read. This means either that they translated it into a more understandable language (probably Aramaic for the exiles), or else they explained its meaning. This, of course, was the role of the priests and Levites: to educate the people in the Torah (see Leviticus 10:10-11). But, once again, to make some connection between this verse and an alleged unbroken chain of binding tradition is to build a mountain out of a non-existent mole hill. Also, the context makes it absolutely clear that the center of attention and authority was the written Word alone—as emphasized in the numerous verses just cited. The rest of Nehemiah 8 also shows us that the Jewish people then did what the Law literally told them to do, without any extra traditions or interpretations added on. And so, Nehemiah 8:15 says that the Jews followed what was written in Leviticus 23:37-40. They obviously had no clue that the Talmud would later claim that Leviticus 23 could not be understood without all kinds of special interpretations and specific traditions.

12. See, for example, Leviticus 24:10-23; Numbers 9:1-14; 15:32-36; 27:1-5; Zechariah 7.

13. *Form of Prayers for Day of Atonement,* rev. ed., (New York: Rosenbaum and Werbelowsky, 1890), 287-88.

CHAPTER 8
BY RANDY AND TRICIA HORNE

CHAPTER 8

It Was Not for Me

Tricia: Why did Jesus have to die for my sins? Raised as a Catholic, this concept was still foreign to me. Everyone knows if you're a good person, you'll go to Heaven when you die. So why did Jesus have to die? It seemed odd. It didn't fit the character of God—or did it? Since I had little knowledge of the Hebrew Scriptures, Jesus' death in exchange for our salvation didn't make much sense to me. But God was about to use a young Jewish man named Randy to draw me into a relationship with Him.

At the time I met Randy, I had been in a period of seeking God for answers. The two questions that bothered me most were: Why did I have terrible back pain? and Why didn't God answer my prayers to heal it? I would go to Mass, pray, pick up the missalette, and skip over all the traditional prayers just to get to God's Word. I knew the Scriptures were the real thing, what church should be all about. But I would kneel, stand, genuflect, bless myself, and do other religious things out of respect.

> **Little did I know that my mother (a quiet believer) had been listening regularly to a radio program called *Messianic Vision*.**

What did Randy have to do with all this? Little did I know that my mother (a quiet believer) had been listening regularly to a radio program called *Messianic Vision*. One day Sid Roth, the host of the program, said on the air, "The Jewish person that God has put in your life is no accident." My mother thought, *That's nice. But I don't know any Jewish people that well.* Within a matter of a few weeks, I told her I had met a nice Jewish guy. Immediately, she made the connection, but she told me nothing about it at the time. After we had been dating for seven or eight months, I told my mother I didn't know how we could pursue marriage with Randy being Jewish and me, Catholic. She suggested I check out the local Messianic Jewish congregation and start listening to Sid Roth's program. When she explained who Sid was, I thought, *A Jewish person who believes in Jesus. How unique.* But was it really? Paul, Peter, Matthew, Mark, John, Stephen—what were these men? Protestants? Catholics? Greek Orthodox? *No.* They were all *Jewish. OK*, I thought, *I'll tune in to this program on the way to work.* After all, this might be a compromise that would work for us. Maybe

Randy could be one of these Jewish people who believes in Jesus.

Jesus, You Loved Me That Much?

So I started listening to testimony after testimony of Jews and Gentiles touched by the powerful love of God. I would weep; I couldn't get enough. I was hungry for truth—for God. I sent for teaching tapes, testimonies, and Bibles. It was all so wonderful. I began to be convicted of sin in my life. The depth and weight of it was suddenly very heavy. I knew I needed pardoning; my sin was coming between me and God.

At the same time, I was listening to Sid and others explaining God's plan of salvation. From the very beginning, God required an atonement, a sacrifice for man's sins. Israel's sacrificial system in the Old Testament was a foreshadowing of Jesus atoning for my sins. Wow! No one is righteous, not one; all of us have gone astray, each one has turned to his own way, but God has laid the iniquity of all of us on Jesus (see Isa. 53:6). This is a better, more excellent way than the Temple sacrificial system because it brings us into a relationship with God.

> **This is a better, more excellent way than the Temple sacrificial system because it brings us into a relationship with God.**

Jesus, you loved me that much? I found myself crying out to God and asking Him for forgiveness one day in the car while tuned in to *Messianic Vision* on my way to work. So began my new life with God. I couldn't stop thinking about Him; I wanted all I could get. From religion I knew about Him and even believed in Him. But now I *knew Him.* What a difference!

In contrast, Randy didn't seem to care whether He even existed. Could we actually pursue marriage like this? Where should I go for advice?

The source who first shared the Gospel with me seemed like a good place to start. Being a new believer with a lot of chutzpah, I called Sid and told him my situation. He said, "No, you can't marry this man, but you can continue to pray that God will show him the truth." That answered that question.

What was God doing in Randy's life?

Randy: I was brought up in a reformed Jewish home. I went to Hebrew school three times a week for six years mainly to prepare for my bar mitzvah. Our family celebrated the high holy days out of tradition rather than out of Torah observance. I always wondered, *What is the sense of any of this?* I had the impression that most of the people present were there just because it was what Jewish people did on these holidays. Hebrew school was not something I enjoyed; for me it was a burden worse than public school because it cut into all of my after-school activities.

> **I don't remember a single time
> asking myself if I thought God
> existed or asking Him who He was.**

I should have been seeking answers to questions about who God was and how He related to my life. But I was so caught up in sports, who *I* was, where *I* was going, and how *I* would get there, that God never was an issue. I don't remember a single time asking myself if I thought God existed or asking Him who He was. My bar mitzvah was a fun time. I remember studying hard so as not to make a mistake. I got my wish and made it through without any flaws. Not making a mistake was much more important to me than the ceremony or any other part of my bar mitzvah. In my family, the bar mitzvah was the pinnacle of each child's Jewish studies. Once you went through this door, you no longer had to attend Hebrew school. As a family, we still attended high holiday services together, but for me it remained hollow and meaningless. The deepest questions I faced at that time were *Why am I at this service?* and *When can I leave?*

Someone Was Listening

That all changed in the summer after I graduated from college, while vacationing on Cape Cod. I met Tricia, whom God would use to change my life from shallowness to one of truly caring about people.

After months of trying to persuade Tricia to yield to my ways, I finally realized it was much easier to yield to hers. Though Tricia was a Catholic, the only thing this meant to me was that she went to church and I didn't. I had very little knowledge about her religion. At this point in my life, I did not attend any religious services other than the dinners my parents held at their house during the Jewish holidays. My understanding of God had not changed—He didn't bother me (or so I thought), and I didn't bother Him.

As Tricia and I started to get more serious about our relationship, religion became more of an issue. Instead of going out with my friends one Friday night, she suggested we attend a Messianic Jewish congregation. I wanted to refuse, but I didn't feel like fighting about it, so I agreed. The service was very Jewish, but different from anything I had experienced. I had never been exposed to individual and corporate spontaneous prayer. It was obvious as these people prayed that they knew someone was listening. The people were nice, but it was not for me.

> **It was obvious as these people prayed that they knew someone was listening.**

We did not return for five months. Neither of us had accepted Jesus as Lord and Savior at this point, although Tricia was truly searching. Then, in the summer of 1985, Tricia gave her life to the Lord. In September she asked me what I was doing for the high holidays. When I told her I didn't have plans since my family was celebrating in New

York with relatives, she suggested we go back to Ruach Israel to see what a Messianic service was like for the holidays. Once again, I agreed.

This time the service was not as foreign to me. Some parts were vaguely familiar, and I even remembered some of the chants. Tricia enjoyed the service so much she wanted us to start attending on a regular basis. We worked out a system where we would meet at a location halfway between our workplaces, park one of the cars, and take the other to the meeting on Friday nights. Many times I would try to convince her that after a long week of work we should skip the service and go somewhere to relax, but to no avail. She would reply, "You can do that, but I really want to attend the services."

After a few weeks of attending, I thought I might as well try and get something out of it, so I began to listen more attentively and even started to read the Bible. Before bed I would pray to God and ask Him to show Himself to me. Sometimes I would say "in Jesus' name" to see if anything would happen. As time went on, I learned more about God. But I still had no relationship with Him.

My Neck Has Been Healed!

Sid Roth came to speak at the Copley Place Hotel in Boston on Saturday, April 26, 1986. Tricia had been avidly listening to him on the radio and now of course wanted to attend his meeting. In my mind, we had already gone to service Friday night, and now she wanted to ruin Saturday too. I protested. She persisted.

We went to hear this man speak about how he came to know Jesus and how God had restored his mind and marriage. I thought this was interesting, but I had heard others say the same thing before on the tapes Tricia had been giving me. Near the end of the night, he called people forward who needed to be healed. Tricia went forward for her back, and I went with her. Standing next to Tricia at the front was a woman whom I had met earlier in the week at a Passover seder. I knew she did not believe in Jesus. I came to find out later that the only reason she was there was because it was her husband's birthday, and all he wanted was for her to come and hear Sid. This woman had been in a very serious car accident and could not move her neck. She wore a TENS unit hooked to her neck to stimulate nerve endings to help with the pain. Sid went down the line praying for people, and, of course, they were falling over just like you would see on television. When he got to this woman and Tricia, they didn't fall over, and then the next person in line did. I had it all figured out. He must be paying these people to fall over, and I knew Tricia and this woman were not part of it.

After Sid was finished praying, he said he felt that someone had been supernaturally healed, so he told the people to very slowly move the area in their body that needed healing to check it out. My eyes first went to Tricia. Then I saw the woman next to her shaking her neck and shouting, "My neck! My neck! I can move my neck!"

Although I did not understand what was happening, I knew I had encountered the presence of God, and my life would never be the same.

At that point it almost seemed like I disappeared, because I started to weep—not just shed a tear, but really weep. Although I did not understand what was happening, I knew I had encountered the presence of God, and my life would never be the same.

The next morning I remember waking up and looking at the ceiling and thinking something was very different. Everything was the same, but the way I was looking at it was 180 degrees different from the way I had seen it a day earlier. I later asked Tricia what had happened to me the night before that could make such a difference. She stated calmly, "You had a born-again experience."

I started reading the Bible again and found that passages I couldn't understand before now made complete sense. I was a changed man. Jesus was for me!

Randy and Tricia were married on July 18, 1987, in a beautiful Messianic Jewish ceremony. They now have two children: Daniel Joseph, born July 4, 1990; and Joshua Michael, born November 21, 1993, and are raising them up to love and serve the Messiah of Israel. The Lord has significantly healed Tricia's back, and she leads a normal life free from the agony of back pain.

Commentary by Sid Roth

Randy and Tricia Horne are typical of the many couples who have intermarried. The Jewish community has done research predicting that if intermarriage and assimilation trends continue, there will be very few Jewish people left in America.

Not to worry. God says as long as this earth exists there will be physical Jews (see Jer. 31:35, verse 36 in some versions).

I see something far deeper in the union of Jew and Gentile in marriage. The one-flesh unity of Randy and Tricia reflects the shalom that will make us all one (Jew and Gentile) under the banner of Messiah's love. The rabbis say Jesus is the Messiah of the Gentiles, and we Jews are still waiting for our Messiah. Isaiah 11:10 says from the root of Jesse (David's father) will the Messiah come as a sign to the Gentiles (nations). In other words, the Gentiles will follow the Jewish Messiah.

We Jews believe in one God and one Messiah. Now if the rabbis say Jesus is the Gentile Messiah—by logic that makes Him the Jewish Messiah!

Besides, how can we have peace on earth unless the whole world follows the same Messiah?

Come quickly, Lord Jesus.

CHAPTER 9
BY BATYA SEGAL

CHAPTER 9

Bat Shalom: Daughter of Zion

At the beginning of this century rumors began to circulate that a Jewish State was about to be reborn in the land of our forefathers. Excitement swelled in the Jewish community in Yemen as they felt the days of the Messiah were soon to come. Many Jewish people started to make their way back to Zion. Leaving everything behind except their most essential belongings, they set out on the long perilous journey across the desert, some carrying their children on their shoulders. They had little food or drink. Many suffered from exhaustion, and many died—but they died full of hope and faith, knowing they were returning to the land of their forefathers.

In the late 1930s, my father left Yemen for Israel (then called Palestine), traveling by boat from Yemen to Egypt, and from there by train. Most of the family had died either in Yemen or on the way to Israel. Upon arrival in Israel my father joined his one surviving brother. About this same time, my mother and her family settled in Jerusalem.

> **After the rebirth of Israel, the new government committed itself to bringing back the Jewish people from all over the world.**

During the 1948 War of Independence, my father joined the Jewish forces fighting for the survival of the newly born Jewish State of Israel. He served in Ramat Rachel, a kibbutz just south of Jerusalem. After the rebirth of Israel, the new government committed itself to bringing back the Jewish people from all over the world. In 1950, an airlift called *Operation Magic Carpet* brought home to Israel a large part of the Yemenite Jewish community within a short period of time. Most of them had never even seen an airplane before. The rabbi explained from Isaiah 40:31 that God would lead them *"on wings like eagles,"* which dispersed any fears they may have had of flying, for they knew prophetically they were being taken home to be prepared for the days of redemption.

He Hears Your Prayers

The Israeli Yemenite Jewish community in which I was raised was Orthodox. My parents kept a kosher home and were strict observers of *Torah* (the five books of Moses). They kept the *Shabbat* (Sabbath) and all the feasts of Israel.

As I grew up, I went to an Orthodox girls' school in our neighborhood. Every morning we prayed as our forefathers had for two thousand years. At school we learned about the Messiah, who would come and redeem the Jewish people. He would reveal to the world that the God of Israel is the true God and would bring peace to all nations. He would sit on His throne in Jerusalem and rule the world with an iron rod. Though we learned this, the emphasis in our school was on the *Dinim*, the laws and commandments we had to follow as observant Jews. It was not a subject that excited us very much. I could not understand how it would bring me to a closer and deeper understanding of God, but I knew from studying the Jewish prophet, Isaiah, that God's thoughts were higher than my thoughts, so I didn't argue.

My father read his Bible every day when he returned from work. He instilled in me a love for and firm belief in God and His Word.

The atmosphere at home was warm, loving, and full of music. When we came together with family and friends on Shabbat, holidays, and special occasions, we sang and prayed according to the Yemenite traditions.

My father read his Bible every day when he returned from work. He instilled in me a love for and firm belief in God and His Word. He taught me, "Never forget that God exists. Whenever you need Him, for whatever reason, then

He is always there to help you. Turn to God because He hears your prayers, and He knows your needs."

Every evening before I went to sleep, my father and I quoted together a passage of Scripture I knew by heart:

> *Sh'ma Yisrael, Adonai Elohenu, Adonai Echad. Ve-Ahavta Et Adonai Eloheicha Bechol Levavcha Uv'chol Nafshecha Uv'chol me-odech .... ["Hear, O Israel: The Lord our God, the Lord is one. Love the Lord your God with all your heart, with all your soul, and with all your might ..."]* (Deuteronomy 6:4-9 NKJV).

I followed this with a personal talk with God. I used to bring before Him all the things of the day about which I was concerned, and I had the assurance that He heard my prayers and was meeting my needs. I knew God was my Father in Heaven, and I loved Him, but there were aspects of His character—His righteousness, holiness, and judgment—I did not understand, and so I feared Him as well.

As a child I loved art and got good grades in painting and drawing. I also was very interested in theatre and had the opportunity to act in some productions. I began to attend a children's group at the main radio station of Israel where we read stories and sketches on the radio. I loved it. This opened a whole new world for me. The director said I had an excellent voice for radio, and he could help me to make this my profession when I graduated.

My father would tell me, "Don't spread yourself so thin. Concentrate on one thing, and do it well." I knew this was very good advice, but I loved all I did, and it was difficult for me to give up anything.

I had the support and love of both my parents; my father, in particular, always encouraged and complimented me. Of course, the youngest child generally gets the most attention, so at times I was spoiled.

Miracle War

As I was preparing to finish elementary school and begin the summer holidays in June 1967, Israel suddenly found herself embroiled in what became known as the Six Day War. Israelis remember it as the "Miracle War." I was surprised to see that both of my brothers and my father were called to serve in the reserves. For seven days our family sat in the neighbor's basement, anxiously waiting to hear the news. Our only contact with the outside world was the radio. Every hour, when we heard the beep, we ran to listen to the latest bulletins.

> Israelis remember it as the "Miracle War." ...For seven days our family sat in the neighbor's basement, anxiously waiting to hear the news.

On the second day of the war, all the adults in the room began jumping with joy, hugging each other, and shouting. When I asked why, I was told that Jerusalem had been reunited, and our Israeli flag had been lifted on the

Temple Mount. Even as a child I realized this was a miracle only God could have performed. After two thousand years of foreign domination, Israel had expanded her borders to the heartland of her ancient territory! I began to understand God's prophetic word for the Jewish people.

I Need Freedom

When I was 12 years old and in a secondary school, I started to question my way of life. I began to break away from the teachings of my youth and go my own way. Since I greatly respected my parents and did not want to hurt them, I waited for the appropriate time and then explained my feelings to them. "I can't live this way anymore," I said. "I respect your lifestyle, but I need to explore a different one for me. I believe very strongly in God, but the *mitzvot* (laws) that I have been taught seem old-fashioned and not suitable for life today. I find I am unable to keep them with my whole heart, and I do not feel they bring me closer to God." I asked for their permission to go to a public high school.

My father has always been an open-minded man, so he said: "It is all right. You can do that as long as you are happy. But do not forget who your God is and where you come from."

And so I transferred to public school. This proved to be a great challenge. I was confronted with a totally different culture. And much to my surprise, some teachers, including the head teacher, did not believe in the Bible as the Word of God. Instead, they viewed the Bible as a collection of mythical tales not really inspired by God.

> **He singled out one boy in our class, who wore a *kippah,* as the object of sarcastic remarks and ridicule.**

An even greater shock was finding that one of my teachers was an avowed atheist and particularly sharp toward any student who believed in God. He singled out one boy in our class, who wore a *kippah,* as the object of sarcastic remarks and ridicule.

My frustrations at this new school challenged me to study the Bible for myself. It was an eye-opening experience to study the books of Isaiah, Ezekiel, Jeremiah, and the other prophets. The prophecies concerning the return of the Jews to our homeland amazed me.

Because of my disenchantment over the way the Bible and other subjects were taught, I began to question the wisdom of attending public school. After two and one-half years, I left and enrolled in a school at which I could study mostly at home and go to classes just two days each week.

This was a period of deep soul-searching for me, a time of seeking for truth. Since I was studying at home, I had a lot of time to think and read. I knew I had not found satisfaction in a religious Orthodox lifestyle, even though I appreciated and identified with the traditions. But I had to ask myself, If keeping the commandments does not bring me peace and a closer relationship with God, then what does? I was searching for the answers to other questions as well: What is the purpose of my life here on earth? Who is God, really? What will happen to me after I die?

I tried to find answers in philosophical books, but they left me confused, raising more questions than answers. I gained no satisfaction from studying them.

Yom Kippur War

My quest for truth was suddenly interrupted by the Yom Kippur War in 1973. This was the hardest war Israel had ever faced. All our Arab neighbors attacked us, declaring a Holy War for Allah, on the holiest day of the Jewish year. Their sole intent was to destroy Israel and annihilate the Jewish population. We were totally unprepared, and consequently this war was a terrible tragedy for us. In Israel, in time of war, all reserve units are called up to strengthen the army. My two brothers and my father were again fighting in a war they had not wanted. Unlike 1967, this became a very personal war to me, as many of my friends and neighbors were either wounded or killed. I was devastated and in deep mourning. I cried to God for answers.

In January 1974, I began my military service, which every Israeli teenager enters at age 18. I served in the navy. It was just after the Yom Kippur War, and I saw some of my friends and acquaintances coming home wounded, some very severely, from the war. This increased my longing to know God and to know what the hereafter had in store for me. I asked all sorts of questions, but never received any clear answers.

Premature Marriage

I had served in the navy for one year when I married and obtained a release from service. A release was generally granted to girls getting married and starting a home. My husband, Avi, was an old friend I had known before I went into the navy. He was six years older than I and a confirmed atheist.

I still do not know what induced me to marry. As I reflect on it now, I realize I was far too young and made an impulsive decision. However, there was a lot of confusion in those days and emotions were blown out of proportion. I had lost friends in the war and felt I was in danger of losing another. Even though the marriage was a mistake, I know God was watching over my life.

Our relationship fell apart after only one year. After giving up all hope that our marriage would ever amount to anything, we agreed to separate. But the day we decided to get a divorce, Avi had to go to the Galilee on a press assignment (he was a press photographer). On the way back he was involved in a serious traffic accident in which his friend, the driver of the car, was killed, and Avi was seriously injured. It was a miracle he came out of the wreckage alive. He suffered a severe concussion, which the doctors told him would require a long period of rest. Ironically, just a few days after the accident, I discovered I was pregnant. Because of Avi's injuries and my pregnancy, we decided to stay together. When he left the hospital, however, Avi went to his mother's home for several months to recuperate.

Transcendental Meditation

Meanwhile, I was under tremendous pressure. I was 20 years old, pregnant with my first baby, and in a marriage hanging together by a thread. I was trying to earn a living and at the same time visit my husband in the hospital every day. I had to travel from Jerusalem to Tel Aviv, and then spend hours in the intensive care unit. Since I could not really communicate with Avi, I would sit and watch the injured soldiers entering the hospital. One had been explaining to his friends how to dismantle a hand grenade when it exploded in his face. His brain had died, but his heart kept beating. I saw others die or remain comatose.

> **I was under tremendous pressure.**
> **I was 20 years old, pregnant with**
> **my first baby, and in a marriage**
> **hanging together by a thread.**

Again I was caught in a web of circumstances that forced me to think about issues of life and death. I knew there had to be answers to my questions—answers that would change my life. I also knew I would have no peace until I found them.

I got a part-time job working for the Ministry of the Treasury. While there, I made friends with a lady deeply involved in transcendental meditation (TM). She knew I was going through a hard time and encouraged me to come to their meetings, believing they held the answer for me. In my desperation, I finally yielded to her persuasions and let her enroll me in a course. I had been very concerned this might be a religion, despite her assurance it wasn't. However, toward the end of the course, my friend said, "I forgot to tell you, there is a closing ceremony, but you can ignore what takes place." This aroused my curiosity.

We were told to bring an apple and a new white handkerchief as an offering for the maharishi (though I did not realize at first what was taking place). One by one we were taken into a small room with a TM instructor who stood in the back whispering incantations while the incense smoke arose by the picture of the guru. I laid down my apple as an offering to the maharishi. Then the instructor gave me my own special mantra to repeat while meditating.

The ceremony made me very uncomfortable, and I went home in despair. This was in stark contrast to TM's promises of personal fulfillment, joy, peace, and contentment. I tried to ignore the religious part of the course and continued doing the exercises and the early morning meditations as I believed it would help me in my pregnancy.

> **Then suddenly it hit me: "By doing TM, I'm worshiping other gods!"**

I knew something was wrong, but I could not put my finger on it. Then suddenly it hit me: "By doing TM, I'm worshiping other gods!" Once I understood the implications, I was almost physically sick. I confronted my TM friend: "You said this wasn't a religious course, but now I realize I was ensnared in idolatry!"

A New Profession

As time went by, Avi improved physically. He started working a few hours a day in his lab, but was frustrated with his physical limitations and inability to provide properly for his family. He became self-absorbed and lost his temper easily. It was difficult to communicate with him. After the dreadful experience of TM and with my married life deteriorating, I turned more and more to God with my questions, crying out to Him for comfort, appealing to Him for help in my distress, and begging Him to reveal Himself to me.

> **After the dreadful experience of TM and with my married life deteriorating, I turned more and more to God with my questions, crying out to Him for comfort, appealing to Him for help in my distress, and begging Him to reveal Himself to me.**

When trouble comes, it does not seem to stop. Avi broke the metal plate in his hip and had to be rushed to the hospital. He had an emergency operation and once again was confined to the hospital for several months. This time he had a plaster body cast. He was admitted to a private hospital close to home, so I didn't have to travel as far to visit him.

Through Avi's long-term illness, I had taken on the responsibility of supporting the family, but I was only working part-time at the Ministry of Treasury, so I began to look for a second job.

It was at that time that God began to answer my prayers. A friend of ours knew of a printing business looking for a computer typist to operate a typesetting machine. One day he called us to see how we were doing. He asked if I knew of anyone looking for a part-time job. "Yes, I know someone—me," I said. "But I have no training in typesetting."

He quickly replied, "That doesn't matter. If you take the job, they will train you!"

"Then I'll take it," I announced. "I would love to learn a new profession." Little did I know what God had in mind.

From my first day at the printing firm, I knew I was part of something very special. There was a wonderful atmosphere, and the few people I saw were very kind to me. Even the interview with the manager was pleasant.

Although I started out with no knowledge of computers, after a while I became quite proficient. I worked in a tiny room where I operated one computer and Ibrahim, a young Beduin Arab, operated the other. He was about my age, 23, married, and already had four children.

A Different New Testament

One morning my employer handed me an envelope with a manuscript for me to typeset. When I pulled it out, I discovered it was the New Testament in Hebrew. My first reaction was, "Oh no, this can't be real! What sort of place is this? Why do they want to print the New Testament in Hebrew here? Are they missionaries?"

For a while I sat there struggling with my conscience: *What* chutzpah *(nerve) they have! Shall I do it? What am I supposed to do?* My mind whirled. I needed the job, but how could I work on such a thing? I felt I had no choice, so I began. It was difficult to open the manuscript and start typing, thinking I was contributing to the work of missionaries, helping them convert Jewish people and steal Jewish souls. I vividly recalled a story I had read as a child about a widow named Hannah who had seven children. She lived during the time of the Inquisition. When faced with the choice of death or bowing to the cross, she heroically refused to yield, choosing death rather than conversion.

> **The longer I worked on the manuscript, the clearer it became to me the New Testament was a Jewish book!**

As I began to type and read the New Testament, it was different than I had expected. To my amazement, on the first page was the genealogy of Yeshua, which showed Him to be a descendant of Abraham of the line of David. My first discovery was that Yeshua was a Jew! And the disciples were Jews! The longer I worked on the manuscript, the clearer it became to me the New Testament was a Jewish book! Then the questions began. *What's wrong with it?* I thought. *Why are the rabbis so against it? Why do they reject this book?* All these questions went through my mind while typing.

I had been brought up to believe that Jesus was the God of the Christians and that the New Testament was a Christian book, yet I knew I was typesetting a book that was completely Jewish. How could this be? And if Christians followed a Jewish book, how could they have persecuted the Jewish people for so many centuries? And so the struggle for my salvation began. My heart was no longer at peace. In my head it made sense to me that Yeshua was the Jewish Messiah, but my upbringing kept my heart from accepting that idea. As I read the words of Yeshua in *HaBrit HaHadashah* (the New Testament), truth began to shine into my life. Yeshua said all actions stem from a person's heart, and God is concerned with our thoughts and motives—not just our actions. That really struck home.

> **Then came the amazing revelation of eternal life. I thought, *This is the answer I have been seeking for a long, long time.* … The words of Yeshua pierced to the very depths of my heart, and although I was still fighting, God was winning the battle.**

Then came the amazing revelation of eternal life. I thought, *This is the answer I have been seeking for a long, long time. All I have known up until now has been very obscure concerning eternal life, but Yeshua's words are very clear and certain, and I can understand them.* The words of Yeshua pierced to the very depths of my heart, and although I was still fighting, God was winning the battle.

Is This Truth?

Two major questions remained: Is this really the truth, or am I deceiving myself? and Why does the name of Yeshua generate so much anger among the Orthodox Jews?

I began to look up the references in the *Tanakh* (the Old Testament) to check them against quotations in the Gospels. I wanted to know if the prophecies and promises of Yeshua's coming were really written in the Tanakh. I delved deeply into the subject.

After many months of searching, I felt I could go no further without help. So I began to ask all my friends, "Who is the Messiah really?" "Why hasn't the Messiah come yet?" "Why couldn't Yeshua be the Messiah?" I bombarded everyone I met with my questions, even people I hardly knew. I was not ashamed, but was very open about it.

Still I had doubts about whether Yeshua was Messiah. Sometimes I felt as if I had found a great treasure, but a little later, I would dismiss it again. My turmoil lasted for months.

During this time, Avi was discharged from the hospital and came back to live with me again as we had decided to give our marriage another chance. While he had almost recovered from his initial concussion, his legs were still in casts.

After I had finished typing the New Testament, I was given various Christian books to typeset in Hebrew. These included *The Hiding Place,* a book about Corrie ten Boom, a Christian who had hidden Jews during the Holocaust; *Run Baby Run,* the story of Nicky Cruz, a New York gang leader whose life was changed by faith in Yeshua; and *Joni,* the story of Joni Erikson, whose faith had sustained her when she became a quadriplegic as the result of a swimming accident. Those books made a great impression on me. While I was working on the computer, tears would sometimes run down my cheeks. I saw how God's love had touched people and radically changed their lives.

I See an Angel

About nine months after I had started typesetting the New Testament and the other books into Hebrew, I was troubled more than ever with my many questions. But no one I asked was able to give me satisfactory answers.

One night in desperation I went to my bedroom and cried out to God: "God, please show me the way I should go. Is Yeshua the true Messiah of Israel, or is He a false Messiah? If He is the true Messiah, I want to follow Him and serve Him. But if He is not, please let me forget about Him."

Right after I prayed, I saw a vision of a man clothed in a long white robe. His bearded face was shining and full of glory. The countenance of the man was majestic. I did not understand the meaning of this vision, yet I felt God was trying to give me a sign.

> **"God, please show me the way I should go. Is Yeshua the true Messiah of Israel, or is He a false Messiah? If He is the true Messiah, I want to follow Him and serve Him. But if He is not, please let me forget about Him."**

The next day I left work at 3:00 P.M. and was standing at the bus stop watching for the next bus. Suddenly, I saw a man coming toward me from the other side of the street. I realized I had seen him before. He had the same face, the same long hair, the same beard, and the same clothes as the man I had seen in the vision the night before. A shock ran through my body, and the experience gave me goose bumps. I looked around to see if anyone else at the bus stop saw him, but no one indicated noticing him. As I looked back toward him, I saw that he had disappeared.

I realized this was God's sign. The tall, bearded man was the man in my vision. It couldn't be a coincidence, my meeting the same man from the vision in the street. I knew it was an angel, and I rejoiced!

At last I was convinced Yeshua was the Messiah. I had total peace and an overwhelming joy in my heart. The struggles between my head and my heart were over. I was thrilled to know I was finally on the right path. This was my turning point.

> **At last I was convinced**
> **Yeshua was the Messiah.**
> **I had total peace and an**
> **overwhelming joy in my heart.**

When I got home, I was so excited about what I had seen, I blurted out to my husband, "Do you know what has just happened? I had a vision, and after that I saw an angel, and he was from God. Yeshua is the Messiah. I'm certain of it!" The revelation was so real to me; I did not consider anyone might doubt it. But Avi, a confirmed atheist, looked at me mockingly as if I had gone crazy. He made fun of me in front of my friends. When he had an attentive audience, he would say sarcastically, "Have you heard? Batya saw an angel, and now she believes in Yeshu!" (This is a derogatory name for Yeshua.) On those occasions I wished the ground would swallow me.

When we were alone I would say to him, "You just don't do that sort of thing! This is something personal, something intimate. You can't ridicule prayer and the things that I experienced with God. This is something between me and God."

I Lose My Daughter

Our relationship continued to deteriorate. I was very vulnerable as a new believer in Yeshua. I had no idea what direction my life would take nor much inner certainty about the future. I needed brothers and sisters in the Body of Messiah to support me. But Avi forbade me to meet with other believers or to read the Bible.

"If you continue doing this," he told me, "I shall fight you in the highest courts and take our daughter away from you."

True to his word, Avi moved ahead with his vendetta. I was ordered to appear before the Rabbinical Court. When Avi arrived, I noticed he was carrying a briefcase. I had no idea what was in it. My lawyer, a religious man, could not guess either. When he came before the judge, Avi opened the case and produced all the books I had typed, plus my New Testament.

"These are her books," he shouted, pointing at me.

"She is a missionary! And I won't have her bringing up my daughter!" There was a great commotion in the courtroom. The rabbis seemed gravely concerned.

After consultation, they forbade Avi to allow me into the house and said that I could no longer raise my daughter. They gave him full custody. My lawyer requested a recess, but they refused. I shouted at the rabbis before I left the courtroom, "God is the only Judge. He will make the decision about where my daughter will be. If God wishes for her to be with me, He will make it possible." My courage to speak amazed me. I almost felt as though the Lord had spoken those words through me.

> **I hugged and kissed my daughter
> good-bye and closed the door of my
> house behind me. I had been banished.**

With a heavy heart and tears streaming down my face, I hugged and kissed my daughter good-bye and closed the door of my house behind me. I had been banished. Defeated. I couldn't understand why God had allowed it to happen.

Yeshua, Please Help!

"Lord," I cried, "this is too much for me. Please help me! I cannot bear this!" With my mouth I said that I was sacrificing my Isaac as Abraham had, but my heart was not in it. She was my daughter! I was leaving my daughter! It felt as though a sword were piercing my soul. I cried, "Oh, Yeshua, please help me!" Amazingly, the separation from my daughter lasted only three days. A finding by the civil court annulled the verdict of the religious court because of a technical error. But I knew it was a miracle from God.

My daughter was with me again! I could take her in my arms and hold her. By the grace of God, I have been able to bring her up, and she is still living with me to this very day. She is now 18 years old and about to enter the Israeli Army. I am proud of her and love her very, very much. The battle in the courts for custody of Tali lasted eight years, including about four years in the Supreme Court of Israel. Year after year it dragged on until Avi decided to marry another woman and pressed me to agree to a divorce.

> **It is amazing how God can use the evil things in the world to bring about good.**

It is amazing how God can use the evil things in the world to bring about good. This fight, which was really persecution for my belief in Yeshua, stimulated my spiritual growth. I had to learn to fight to survive, even though still a baby spiritually. The fight strengthened me, and the problems refined me. The Lord gave me many insights, and my relationship with Him became very deep and secure.

A few years later I became involved with a group of believers who were musicians; we would meet to sing and pray. One evening, we were praying together in a circle, and when I opened my eyes, I saw a young man who had come in late. There was something very familiar about him, though I had never met him before. After that, I kept running into him in Jerusalem. I learned that his name was Barry, and I found that I enjoyed his sense of humor. Barry's whole life before he came to the Lord had revolved around music. He once had been a professional rhythm and blues musician, a style of music totally alien to me. I had heard such music one time as a child, but did not like it at all. When Barry found Yeshua he gave up his guitar (although later God was to use this talent in ministry for Himself). Barry was one of the best guitarists I had ever heard, and, as I also played guitar, we really got on well together.

As the years went by, Barry and I got to know each other well. He was a constant prayer companion for me in my court battles over Tali. We began to work together and finally came to realize that God had brought us together to be man and wife. We had two wedding celebrations, a traditional Yemenite Jewish wedding and a Messianic celebration. It was a wonderful time for both of us. It was not easy for our parents to accept our faith, but the wedding helped give them some insight, and praise God, they never cut us out of their lives. Barry's father, a traditional, Conservative Jew, does not agree with the ultra-Orthodox position that Messianic Jews are no longer Jews.

My parents know I am a believer in Yeshua, and they accept it. They love Barry, and I am still my father's little girl. They love our children: our daughter Tali, our lovely six-year-old son, Ariel ("Lion of God" and one of the names of Jerusalem), and our beautiful daughter, Liran, who is almost two. My parents get great joy from their grandchildren. We have spent many a Shabbat at their table—a mixture of Yemenite Orthodoxy and Messianic Judaism. As Jewish Orthodox people who have great respect for God and His Word, they express their joy at seeing how God has blessed me with a new family.

Commentary by Sid Roth

The "Lubavitchers" are a sect within traditional Judaism. Many believe their rabbi, Manachem M. Schneersohn, who died in 1994, is the Messiah. This group has a synagogue in Siberia.

The president of this synagogue recently visited a local church in his area because he was friends with the pastor. At this meeting there was a Messianic Jewish dance group comprised of Jews, Gentiles, men, women, African American, white, and Hispanic dancers that touched the synagogue leader deeply. Afterward, he said, "Our traditional worship is dead. Many of our young people are leaving the synagogue. But I feel such joy and life in your worship. I feel God's presence. We want what you have. What is the difference between us?"

The leader of the dance group said, "There is only one difference. Our Messiah is Jesus. He died and rose from the dead 2,000 years ago. Your Messiah is Rabbi Schneerson, whom you expect to rise from the dead. But he has been dead for years and will never come back. What you are experiencing from our dance group comes from their intimacy with God. Without Messiah Jesus it is impossible to have intimacy with God."

After we Jewish people have intimacy with God, then our assignment is to tell Gentiles about the Jewish Messiah. Isaiah says the call of the Jew is to be "a light to the Gentiles [nations]" (Isa. 49:6 NKJV). The assignment of the Gentile believer in Jesus is to tell Jewish people about the Messiah (see Rom. 11:11). And when we all do our job, Messiah will return and usher in an age of peace.

CHAPTER 10
BY MANNY BROTMAN

The Amazing Jewish Book and the God-Shaped Hole in My Soul

And ye shall seek Me, and find Me, when ye shall search for Me with all your heart (Jeremiah 29:13).

One does not have to live too many years before discovering that there exists within a certain emptiness, a void or vacuum that the things of this world can never fill. Neither money nor sex, travel, fame, drugs, titles, possessions, nor any other human accomplishment can fill this emptiness.

I call this vacuum, "the God-shaped hole in my soul." I eventually discovered that this particular void is reserved only for the Creator of the Universe, the God of Abraham, Isaac, and Jacob Himself—to live in each of us personally.

Here, then, is the story of my personal search through religion, academics, sports, business, and the media; my discovery of the Bible—the amazing Jewish book; my coming to understand how to have a personal relationship with God; and my experiencing His abundant life.

I tried *religion.* I had a wonderful religion—Judaism. Both of my parents were Jewish. I attended a Conservative synagogue. I was born a Jew, and I would die a Jew! But somehow, even in the synagogue, the God of Abraham, Isaac, and Jacob seemed to be so far away. I didn't feel that I could live my whole life for only religion.

I tried *academics.* I had honors in scholarship both in high school and college. But I could not live my life only for a string of doctorate degrees after my name.

I excelled in *sports.* In Philadelphia, I was quarterback of the championship high school football team and pitcher for the winning city baseball team. I had awards in basketball and table tennis. But I couldn't live only for athletic accomplishments and the friends they brought.

I tried the *business* world. I worked my way up from production control, to vice president's assistant, and, eventually, to corporate president. I had a lovely ranch home in a modern Jewish community. Our company had a twin-engine aircraft and a pilot who flew me and the executives who worked for me wherever we wanted to go. But still, I couldn't live my life only for business accomplishments.

And, then, I experienced the *media.* I was Chairman of the Board of Fourth Television Network. We provided programming to 500 cable franchises. For a number of years, I produced and hosted a nationally syndicated daily radio show which aired on 22 stations. I have been interviewed on numerous national television and radio programs across the United States, Canada, and the Middle East, which were broadcast to millions of people. But even being involved with the media could not be the ultimate purpose of my life. There had to be something more.

During the course of my lifetime, I have been privileged to experience many things that other people would like to experience and have not been able to. But none of my accomplishments could ever fill that God-shaped hole within me. One day at the Fairmount Park Recreation Center in Philadelphia (before I had experienced most of the things described above), I met George Gruen, a Jewish Bible believer. George and his wife, Doris, lived their lives on a higher plane than anyone I had ever met. They had true joy, peace, happiness, and a genuine love for me and others. I wondered what made these people so different.

> **There had to be
> something more.**

George was a coach of baseball and basketball teams. Since I loved sports so much, I wanted to participate. Along with the competition, George conducted Bible studies from the Jewish Scriptures for all participating team members. For the first time in my life, I seriously considered the credentials and the message of the Jewish Bible.

The Credentials of the Amazing Jewish Bible

> *Wherewithal shall a young man cleanse his way?*
> *by taking heed thereto according to Thy Word....*
> *Thy Word have I hid in mine heart, that I might*
> *not sin against Thee* (Psalm 119:9,11).

First of all, I discovered that the Jewish Bible is histori-cally accurate when checked against other existing histori-cal records. And, in some cases, it gives the only sensible account for certain periods of time when no other histori-cal records are available.

Then the Jewish Scriptures are geographically reliable and have been confirmed many times over by archaeolo-gists who use the Bible as a "road map" to locate buried cities and historical artifacts. Israeli military leaders some-times use ancient battle routes and follow battle strategies found in the *Tanakh* (Jewish Scriptures) in modern-day warfare against Israel's enemies.

Most amazingly, the Jewish Bible specifically foretold the future with 100 percent accuracy in every instance.

Most amazingly, the Jewish Bible specifically foretold the future with 100 percent accuracy in every instance. The Hebrew Scriptures prophesied of:

1) **The Re-establishment of the State of Israel**

In Isaiah 11:12, God said,

*And He shall set up an ensign for the nations,
and shall assemble the outcasts of Israel, and
gather together the dispersed of Judah from the
four corners of the earth.*

God said that He would make Israel like an "ensign" (in Hebrew, "a miraculous flag or banner") for the world to see. He would then re-gather the Jewish people from the four corners of the earth after almost 2,000 years of world-wide dispersion.

On May 14, 1948, Prime Minister David Ben-Gurion stood in Tel Aviv's Museum Hall and proclaimed the Statehood of Israel. A nation was born in a single day exactly as the Bible prophesied over 2,700 years ago (see Isa. 66:8)!

2) The Restoration of Hebrew, "The Pure Language"

In Zephaniah 3:9, it is written,

*For then will I turn to the people a pure language,
that they may all call upon the name of the Lord,
to serve Him with one consent.*

Israel is a "melting pot" of Jewish people from more than a hundred nations of the world; yet, they all learn to speak biblical Hebrew with modern Hebrew words added. One may wonder why Hebrew is called a "pure" language in the Bible. That is because there are no words of vulgarity or profanity in biblical Hebrew!

Never before in the history of mankind has an ancient people been scattered across the face of the earth for almost 2,000 years and later restored to their own land with their own ancient national language. How did the Jewish prophet Zephaniah know that would happen?

3) The Miraculous Defeat of Israel's Enemies in Four Major Wars

Isaiah 19:16-17 predicts the miraculous victories of modern Israel over her enemies, which occurred in 1948 (War of Independence), 1956 (Sinai War), 1967 (Six Day War), and 1973 (Yom Kippur War):

> *In that day shall Egypt be like unto women: and it shall be afraid and fear because of the shaking of the hand of the Lord of hosts .... And the land of Judah shall be a terror unto Egypt ... because of the counsel of the Lord of hosts, which He hath determined against it.*

During the four major wars, Israel's small population of several million Jews had to defend itself time after time against the growing Arab League of 20 nations (now 21 nations) with a population at that time of approximately 140 million Arabs. Israel was outnumbered *5 to 1 in soldiers, 3 to 1 in enemy aircraft and tanks, 8 to 1 in artillery, and 18 to 1 in missiles.* Israel's military budget paled to insignificance when contrasted against the tens of billions of petro-dollars Israel's enemies spent for Israel's destruction. And yet, Israel, even though out-manned, out-gunned, and out-financed, has won war after war against insurmountable odds. *There is no answer but God Himself, who foretold in the Bible this would happen.*

Here are three brief examples of the exciting miracles God performed on behalf of Israel:

A Jewish tour guide testified:

During the war, my men and I were trapped in a minefield. The mines started blowing up all around us. All of a sudden, a little whirlwind of sand appeared and led me and my men through the minefield to safety!

An Israeli wrote me:

I was down in the battlefield and saw on the hilltop a man completely dressed in white helping our soldiers from foxhole to foxhole. Whenever the man lifted his arms up toward heaven, the battle always went in the favor of our Israeli troops. I gave my binoculars to my General to get a better look. He, too, saw the man in white, who then disappeared in front of our eyes!

A reporter told me that his father (also a reporter) was on the Golan Heights after the Israelis captured it. His father asked the Syrian soldiers, "Why did you retreat from the few Jewish soldiers that first came up?" They replied, "You must be mistaken! We did not see a *few* Jewish soldiers. We saw *hundreds* of them!" Whom did these Syrian soldiers see? Did they see the angels of God? Could it be that once again God is sending His angels to fight for His Jewish people and putting a fear in the hearts of Israel's enemies according to Isaiah's prophecy?

4) Agricultural Miracles Would Occur When the Jews Returned to Israel

In Isaiah 35:1, it says,

The wilderness and the solitary place shall be glad for them; and the desert shall rejoice, and blossom as the rose.

When the Jewish people returned to Israel from the four corners of the earth, they found malaria-ridden swamps and parched, barren deserts. The nomads who occupied the land for centuries were not the "children" of the deserts; rather, they were the "fathers" of it. They contributed nothing to restore the land; through their negligence, it had gotten worse. When the Jews returned to their homeland, an agricultural transformation began to take place as prophesied by Isaiah.

When I lived in Chicago, I was able to buy luscious oranges from Israel. In Miami, I could buy tomato juice from Tel Aviv. And, now, in the Washington, D.C. area where I live, I can purchase beautiful fresh-cut flowers from Israel. One only has to visit the famous Carmel Market in Tel Aviv to see the fantastically huge citrus and produce that Israel grows.

The Scripture says, "the desert shall...blossom as the rose." The most important cut flowers that are exported from Israel are roses! The tiny nation of Israel is number three in the world for exporting cut flowers—valued at $140 million a year—with the majority going to Europe. How's that for a dry, parched, barren desert? Bananas, a *warm* climate fruit, are grown in the Jordan Valley with excellent results, while just five miles away, apples, a *cold* climate fruit, also yield a top-quality crop. I have witnessed this marvel with my own eyes.

In the short existence of modern-day Israel, it is already part of a select group of nations that not only produces enough food for its own citizens, but exports 20 percent of its total agricultural products to other countries of the world! Israel also exports its agricultural technology and "know-how" to third-world countries as well as to highly developed countries in Europe and to the United States.

Israel is the most water-efficient country in the world, regulating and controlling alternative water resources such as recycled water from industry and sewage from the domestic sector! Using integrated computerized control of irrigation and fertilization systems in a substantial percentage of Israeli field crops and horticulture minimizes labor costs and maximizes the best possible conditions for the crops. In a special station in Israel's Negev Desert, using desert methods and techniques of irrigation, *salty water* is pumped from the depths of the Negev with unsurpassed results in producing the best tasting and highest quality tomatoes to be found anywhere! Eggplant, yellow melons, potatoes, pears, and table grapes are also watered with this salty water and harvested in the Negev Desert. Once our Jewish people returned to the land, Isaiah's prophecies about flowers in the desert and Israel's agriculture proved to be right on target!

5) Israel's Waste Cities Would Be Rebuilt

The prophet Amos wrote in Amos 9:14,

> *And I will bring again the captivity of My people of Israel, and they shall build the waste cities, and inhabit them; and they shall plant vineyards,*

and drink the wine thereof; they shall also make gardens, and eat the fruit of them.

Since 1948, the Jews have built their nation with one hand and with the other have held their weapons! Despite defending itself in four major wars; caring for the transportation, housing, language-training, employment, and education of millions of immigrants from over a hundred nations; forming a government; and developing an infrastructure, Israel has managed to build and finance a modern nation of which it can be proud!

What once were "waste cities" are now expanding modern cities and ports such as Jerusalem, Tel Aviv, Jaffa, Haifa, and many others. Since its independence, Israel has had a non-stop building program and is reclaiming the desert at such a rate that its map-makers have a hard time staying current. Israel has not only excelled in agriculture, but also in its technology, universities, sciences, defense, medicine, resorts, and much more. The State of Israel is exactly what the Bible said it would be!

6) The Jews Would Return to Israel From the Land of the North (Russia)

Jeremiah 16:14-15 and 23:7-8 tell about Exodus 2:

Therefore, behold, the days come, saith the Lord, that it shall no more be said, the Lord liveth, that brought up the children of Israel out of the land of Egypt; but, the Lord liveth, that brought up the children of Israel from the land of the north ....

If you were to fly north from Jerusalem, you would eventually come to Moscow. The former Soviet Union (especially Russia) contains the only sizable Jewish population north of Israel that could fit this prophecy. It is estimated that there are from two and one-half million (pure-blooded Jews) to ten million (intermarried and "closet" Jews) in the former USSR.

Whatever the numbers, well over a million Russian Jews have already immigrated to Israel in recent years. The majority of these immigrants are highly trained educators, physicians, engineers, and musicians who are infusing Israel with a windfall of intelligent professionals "from the land of the North," exactly as the Jewish Scriptures predicted over 2,600 years ago!

Is it any wonder I call it "The Amazing Jewish Bible?" If one ancient prophecy from the Jewish Scriptures came true, we could call it "luck." If two prophecies came true, we could call it "a lucky coincidence." If three prophecies came true, we could say "what a remarkable lucky coincidence!" But, when prophecy after prophecy after prophecy comes true specifically, by the sheer law of compound probabilities, we have passed from the realms of luck and coincidence, and God has given us a sure word of prophecy that we can live by and upon which we can base our decisions!

I and millions of others have concluded that the Jewish Bible is the most corroborated, authenticated document in the world. Yes, the Bible is confirmed by history, archaeology, geography, prophecy, and the Dead Sea Scrolls. And, most of all, it works in the lives of those who sincerely put it to the test. I can verify this by my own experience. This kind of evidence does demand a verdict. What should we do about it?

I thought it was fascinating, all those years ago, that God fulfilled Bible prophecy, but I wanted to know how that related to me. What was God's plan for me personally?

The Message of the Jewish Bible

> *Come now, and let us reason together, saith the Lord: though your sins be as scarlet, they shall be as white as snow; though they be red like crimson, they shall be as wool* (Isaiah 1:18).

As I searched the Jewish Scriptures, I discovered that God's plan to have my sins forgiven and to have me enter into a personal relationship with Him could be summarized in five spiritual principles. I call these "The Five Jewish Laws." In other words, just as the Creator has well-defined physical laws (such as gravity, centrifugal force, and inertia) that govern the operation of the universe, so He has well-defined spiritual laws that govern our relationship with Him. Here are these laws:

Law 1 Tells of God's *Purpose* ...

> *...God created you and me to have a personal relationship with Himself, and, as a result of that relationship, to enjoy His abundant life!*

Nothing gives God greater pleasure than when you and I choose to have a personal relationship with Him out of our own free will!

> *The Lord hath made all things for Himself [His own pleasure]...* (Proverbs 16:4).

A personal relationship with God will bring you His abundant life of peace, purpose, meaning, joy, and happiness.

> *At thy right hand there are pleasures for evermore* (Psalm 16:11).

This is a wonderful life to have, isn't it? But most people don't seem to be experiencing this abundant life today. Why not? This brings us to Law 2.

Law 2 Reveals Man's *Problem* ...

> *...Sin separates you from a personal relationship with God and His abundant life. Sin also causes spiritual death.*

> *But your iniquities [your sins] have separated between you and your God* ... (Isaiah 59:2).

> *The soul that sinneth, it shall die [spiritual death]* (Ezekiel 18:4).

Sin also causes guilt, unhappiness, lack of peace, frustration, and a lack of purpose. *What is sin? It is the transgression or breaking of God's law.* Part of the *Shema* (Deuteronomy 6:5) says,

> *And thou shalt love the Lord thy God with all thine heart, and with all thy soul, and with all thy might.*

If we do not love God with all of our heart, soul, and might, then we have broken the most important and First Commandment and have sinned. If we put anything before God such as self, material possessions, sex, money, drugs, or anything else, then we have made idols of those things and have committed idolatry. If we hate somebody in our hearts, then we are murderers. If we lust in our hearts, then we are adulterers. If we steal, kill, lie, covet, work on the Sabbath, or dishonor our parents, then we have broken the Ten Commandments. Actually, our rabbis and scholars tell us that there are 613 Commandments in the Tenach that we should all keep.

> ## Who can keep all of these commandments? None of us!

Who can keep all of these commandments? None of us! First Kings 8:46 says,

> *For there is no man that sinneth not ....*

As I studied the Jewish Scriptures, I realized that, both knowingly and unknowingly, I had broken countless commandments of God and that I had to turn from these sins with God's help. Ezekiel 33:11 quotes the Lord God:

> *As I live, saith the Lord God, I have no pleasure in the death of the wicked [unforgiven]; but that the wicked [unforgiven] turn from his way and live: turn ye, turn ye from your evil [sinful] ways; for why will ye die, O house of Israel?*

I realized that I had sinned and needed God's help.

Are you willing to admit that you too have sinned and need God's help? That brings us to Law 3.

Law 3 Explains God's *Plan*...

A) You Cannot Remove Sin by Your Own Human Efforts.

None of us can get to Heaven by keeping the Ten Commandments (the law). The knowledge of sin is produced by God's law, which is so pure and perfect that it is His ruler or measurement to show us, as human beings, how far short we fall of God's glory and holiness. Without the law, we would not even know how sinful we are.

Man's plan is to try to remove his own sins by his own human efforts. These efforts may include religion (man's attempts to reach God) or just plain being "a do-gooder," hoping that one's good deeds outweigh one's bad deeds to attain self-righteousness. In Proverbs 14:12, it says,

> *There is a way which seemeth right unto a man, but the end thereof are the ways of death [spiritual separation from God]!*

Again, the Creator who has put a hundred billion galaxies in space in perfect mathematical and chronological precision is not sloppy when it comes to His spiritual laws. If one does not obey God's precise spiritual laws as revealed and confirmed in His Word, one cannot achieve God's required righteousness (right standing with God).

B) Sin Can Only Be Removed by Faith—Believing What God Says and Acting Upon it.

Righteousness comes by faith. Genesis 15:6 says,

> And he [Abraham, the Father of the Jewish
> People] believed [had faith] in the Lord; and He
> [God] counted it [Abraham's faith] to him for
> righteousness.

Righteousness with God does not come by our good works (*mitzvot*). For by God's grace—something that we don't deserve—you and I are forgiven through faith. It is not of ourselves. It is the gift of God, not of our human works, unless any of us should boast and say that we deserve it (see Eph. 2:8-9).

C) Faith Must Be Placed in God's Provided Blood of Atonement ("Covering" for Sin).

If one has spiritual faith in the sense that the Bible describes, then God requires an act of faith acceptable to Him. Leviticus 17:11 says,

> For it is the blood that maketh an atonement [covering] for the soul.

When the Temple was in existence and the lamb was sacrificed on the altar providing the blood of atonement, this was an act of faith acceptable to God! But, since the Temple is no longer in existence, and the sacrificial system has ceased, how can we have the blood of atonement today by an act of faith? That brings us to Law 4.

Law 4 Shows God's *Provision*...

God has provided the blood of atonement today through a Perfect Sacrifice, One whom the Jewish Bible calls "The Messiah." The word *Messiah* means "The Anointed One."

Isaiah 53:5-6 says:

> *But He was wounded through our transgressions [rebellions], bruised through our iniquities [moral evils]: the chastisement [punishment] of our peace [welfare] was upon Him; and with His wounds [stripes, blood] we are healed [atoned for]. All we like sheep have gone astray [sinned]; we have turned every one to his own way; and the Lord hath caused the iniquity of us all to fall upon Him [the Messiah].*

In the life of Abel (Adam and Eve's son), we see how God provided atonement for *one person* (see Gen. 4:4). On Passover, we see God's atonement for *a family* (see Exod. 12:13).

On Yom Kippur, the Day of Atonement, we see God's provision for *a nation* (see Lev. 16:30).

And, in the Messiah, we see atonement for *all who believe* (have faith) in Him as their personal perfect Passover Lamb (see Isa. 53).

But the critical question is, "How can we know *who* is the true Jewish Messiah?"

In the Scriptures, God gives over 300 prophecies that clearly identify the Messiah. According to the law of compound probabilities, there is only one chance in 33,554,432 that even 25 of these prophecies could be fulfilled by a single person.[1]

Whoever has fulfilled the following prophecies is the true Messiah of Israel. The Messiah would

- be born in Bethlehem of Judah (see Micah 5:1-2).

- be born of a virgin as a miracle sign to the Jewish people (see Isa. 7:14). The Hebrew word for virgin used in Isaiah 7:14 is *almah*. This is translated in some versions of the Bible as "maiden" or "young woman." However, in the Jewish Scriptures, when *almah* is used and read in context, it is almost always clear that it refers to "a virgin." Furthermore, God promised Israel "a sign." It would not be a sign for a normal young maiden to bear a child. It *would* be a sign if a *virgin* gave birth to a child by the hand of God. Please note that the Hebrew name of this Child, *Immanuel,* means, "God with us." This shows His unusual nature. Some stumble at this prophecy because of their lack of faith. God, who put the universe in place, could have easily had a virgin bear a child. Besides, what is that compared to God's marvelous creation of a human being!

- be despised and rejected of men (see Isa. 53:3).

- live a sinless life (see Isa. 53:9).

- be betrayed for 30 pieces of silver (see Zech. 11:12-13).

- die for the sins of the Jewish people and the whole world (see Isa. 53:5-6,8).

- die by crucifixion (see Ps. 22:14-18; Zech. 12:10).

- have his clothing gambled for at the time of His death (see Ps. 22:18).

- come before the destruction of the Second Temple (A.D. 70) (see Dan. 9:24-26).

- arise from the dead (see Ps. 16:10; 110:1).

Only *one man* in history has fulfilled these prophecies. He has changed the calendar and the course of history; and millions of Jews and Gentiles have trusted Him for their personal atonement. His Hebrew name is Yeshua, which means, "salvation." To my non-Jewish friends He is known as "Jesus," which was originally translated from the Greek as Je'sus (hay-SOOS) Christos (CHRIS-tose), and was later anglicized as "Jesus, The Christ," which means, "Salvation, The Messiah"!

When you meet God's requirements concerning Messiah Yeshua, you do not lose your wonderful biblical Jewish heritage; rather, you complete your Judaism by gaining the blood of atonement, gaining the Messiah, and gaining an infinitely more personal relationship with the God of Abraham, Isaac, and Jacob!

However, it is not enough for you just to know intellectually that Yeshua is the Messiah. An act of faith is needed to receive the Messiah's blood of atonement and to enter into God's abundant life. That brings us to Law 5.

Law 5 Gives Man's *Prerogative* (A Free Will Choice)...

...You need to ask Messiah Yeshua into your heart and life in order to have the blood of

atonement and a personal relationship with
God, and to enjoy His abundant life. The
Messiah will not force His way into your life;
He desires to be invited.

Joel 3:5 (2:32 in some versions) states,

> *Whosoever shall call on the name of the Lord
> shall be delivered [saved]!*

Salvation means "deliverance" from sin's penalty (separation from God), sin's power (over you), and, someday, from sin's presence (eternal life)!

When you ask Messiah Yeshua into your heart and life, you will receive His atonement and eternal life. As you grow in Him spiritually, you will experience personal peace, joy, happiness, guidance, meaning, purpose, and much more than you could ever imagine.

I Found the Abundant Jewish Life

> *I am come that they might have life, and that they
> might have it more abundantly (Messiah Yeshua
> in John 10:10 KJV).*

As I studied the prophecies which identified the Messiah, I knew in my heart that only one man in all of history fulfilled them, and He was Yeshua of Nazareth.

Yeshua was born of a virgin in Bethlehem. He lived a sinless life. No one ever found even one sin in Him. History testified that He healed the sick by giving sight to the blind, hearing to the deaf, speech to the dumb, walking to the lame, and cleansing to the lepers. He even raised people from the dead! He was despised and rejected by jealous leaders. He was betrayed for thirty pieces of silver. He died by crucifixion for the sins of the Jewish people and for the whole world. Those who crucified Him gambled for His garments. And He died before the destruction of the Second Temple.

> **History testified that He healed the sick by giving sight to the blind, hearing to the deaf, speech to the dumb, walking to the lame, and cleansing to the lepers.**

The Prophet Daniel wrote that after the "Anointed One" (the Messiah) was "cut off" (murdered), a Prince would come and destroy the city (Jerusalem) and the Sanctuary (the Temple). After Yeshua's death, Prince Titus and the Roman Legions destroyed the city of Jerusalem and the Second Temple in A.D. 70, exactly as Daniel prophesied. Since the Levitical sacrificial system was no longer available, it meant that God had now provided *once and for all time* a perfect atonement through the blood of Messiah Yeshua—for *all* who would believe (see Dan. 9:24-26)!

Yeshua also arose from the dead as King David prophesied. Flavius Josephus, the primary Jewish and Roman historian of that time, wrote in his *Antiquities of the Jews,*

Now, there was about this time Jesus, a wise man, *if it be lawful to call Him a man,* for He was a doer of wonderful works—a teacher of such men as receive the truth with pleasure.... *He was The Messiah*; and, when Pilate, at the suggestion of the principal men amongst us, had condemned Him to the cross, those that loved Him at the first did not forsake Him, for *He appeared to them alive again the third day* [to over 500 Jewish witnesses], as the divine prophets had foretold these and ten thousand other wonderful things concerning Him![2]

Here I was, faced with a dilemma. How could I, as a Jew, accept Yeshua? Would that make me become a *goy*, a "Gentile?" George Gruen pointed out to me that the hope of the Messiah was not of Gentile, but of Jewish origin. It came from the Jewish Bible, and even today observant Jews recite from Moses Maimonides' *Thirteen Principles of the Jewish Faith*: "I believe with perfect faith in the coming of the Messiah; and though He tarry, I will wait daily for His coming!"[3] The question was not whether accepting Messiah was a "Jewish thing" to do—it definitely was—but, rather, *who* is the Jewish Messiah? I had no doubt about who fulfilled all those prophecies! Besides, accepting a Jewish Messiah out of a Jewish Bible and having the Jewish blood of atonement was a very Jewish thing to do. It did sound very kosher! Then, one day, in the privacy of my home, I got on my knees and prayed:

Dear Heavenly Father, I know that I have sinned against You, and I ask Your forgiveness. Messiah Yeshua, please come into my heart and life, cleanse me with Your precious blood of atonement, and make me a child of God. Thank You for doing this according to Your Word. Amen!

When I prayed that prayer, the lights in my room did not flicker. An angel did not knock on my door with a telegram from God. But the God of Abraham, Isaac, and Jacob came closer than my hands or my breath, and I found a peace that passed all understanding and a joy unspeakable and full of glory!

Since that day in Philadelphia, over 40 years ago, the Messiah has not left me. He is a friend who sticks closer than a brother. Everything that God has promised in His Word has come true—love, peace, joy, forgiveness, happiness, guidance, purpose, and so much more! My mother, Ethel, my sisters, Rose and Joyce, and a number of my relatives and friends also invited the Messiah into their lives!

At the age of 19, I married Audrey Yvonne Kitchen. When Audrey was only 6 years old, she contracted Bulbar Polio, the most deadly of the three types of polio. She was completely paralyzed from her neck down to the soles of her feet. She could not move her arms, hands, or legs. She couldn't even swallow her saliva.

Her parents were not yet believers in Yeshua, but her grandparents were strong Bible believers, and volumes of prayer ascended to the throne of God. God reversed the incurable Bulbar Polio and completely healed Audrey! The doctor said it was a miracle! He said there was no way he could explain her recovery medically.

God graciously extended her life another 44 years. Audrey, who hadn't even been able to swallow her own saliva, was given a lovely singing voice to glorify God. She led a very active life as a wife, a mother of two sons, and an outstanding business administrator. We were married for almost 28 years before Audrey went home to Heaven.

In the fullness of God's time, the Lord brought Sandra Frances Sheskin, a beautiful Jewish woman, into my life. Sandra is a first-generation American, born of Jewish immigrant parents from Poland, and raised in a practicing Orthodox Jewish home. Most of her family members, from both sides, were murdered by the Nazis.

Prior to our marriage, Sandra was the main public spokesperson for the United States government on the History and Heritage of the National Emblem of the U.S.A., The Great Seal of the United States. In that position, Sandra was directly responsible to the Office of the President.

Sandra is a Messianic concert singer and recording artist, having shared her love for Israel and her Messiah from Jerusalem to the White House and around the world—and before as many as a million people "live." Together we have been very involved in bringing our Jewish people out of Russia back to Israel, combating anti-Semitism worldwide, and teaching the Jewish Scriptures.

> **Today, there are tens of thousands of Messianic Jews and hundreds of Messianic Jewish synagogues and congregations where Jewish believers worship, with at least 40 such congregations and fellowships in Israel.**

Today, there are tens of thousands of Messianic Jews and hundreds of Messianic Jewish synagogues and congregations where Jewish believers worship, with at least 40 such congregations and fellowships in Israel. Each year, thousands of Bible believers attend Messianic Jewish conferences. What a joy to be involved in this end-time Messianic Jewish spiritual awakening that God promised our people in Hosea 3:5:

> *Afterward shall the children of Israel return, and seek the Lord their God, and David their king [referring to the Messiah]; and shall fear the Lord and His goodness in the latter days.*

There are so many more wonderful things that the Messiah has done in our lives—answers to prayer, miracles of provision, healings of illnesses, supernatural guidance, and much, much more. It would take volumes to write about it.

I cannot encourage you enough to invite Messiah Yeshua into your heart and life.

> *O taste and see that the Lord is good: blessed is the man that trusteth in Him (Psalm 34:9, verse 8 in some versions). Whosoever shall call on the name of the Lord shall be delivered [saved] (Joel 3:5; 2:32 in some versions).*

Here is how to invite Messiah Yeshua into your heart and life as an act of faith to receive His blood of atonement:

1) *Pray:* Prayer is just talking to God in your own words.

2) *Confess*: Acknowledge to God that you have sinned—broken His Commandments—and that you are truly sorry for it.

3) *Ask* and *Receive*: Ask Messiah Yeshua to come into your heart and life and to cleanse you with His blood of atonement.

4) *Believe*: Thank Him by faith for doing this!

Some people have emotional experiences when they invite the Messiah into their life, and others do not. Just thank Him for coming into your heart, not based on human feelings, but on the authority of the Jewish Bible. This is an act of faith acceptable to God! Here is a sample prayer:

> Dear God, I confess that I have sinned against You, and I'm truly sorry for it. Messiah Yeshua, please come into my heart and life and cleanse me with Your precious blood of atonement. Thank You for doing this according to Your Word. I'll do anything You want me to, with Your help. I really mean it, Lord! In Your Name, Amen!

Does this prayer express the desire of your heart? If it does, pray it *right now*, and the Messiah will enter your life as He promised to in God's Word. (You can take a moment right now and pray this prayer out loud.)

Did you invite Messiah Yeshua into your life? Did you really mean it? Then, where is Yeshua according to the Bible? God's Word says,

Behold, I stand at the door [of your heart and life], and knock: if any man hear My voice, and open the door [of his heart and life], I will come in to him, and will sup [fellowship] with him, and he with Me (Messiah Yeshua in Revelation 3:20 KJV).

Either God is the world's greatest liar, or Messiah Yeshua is in your heart right now if you prayed to receive Him!

God is not a man, that He should lie; neither the son of man, that He should repent: hath He said, and shall He not do it? or hath He spoken, and shall He not make it good? (Numbers 23:19).

The moment that you asked Messiah Yeshua into your heart and life as an act of faith, God began to do many wonderful things for you including the following:

1) Your sins were atoned for (covered, forgiven)!

2) You received righteousness (right-standing with God) by faith!

3) You entered into a personal relationship with God and became a child of God!

4) You received eternal life!

5) God's Holy Spirit (*Ruach ha Kodesh*) entered your life to lead you and guide you!

6) You began the abundant life and the exciting adventure for which God created you—to know God and to make Him known!

(If you did not yet ask Messiah Yeshua into your life, ask Him to come in right now, and these wonderful blessings will be yours, too!)

Here's how to grow in God's abundant life:

1) Confess any future sins to God and ask His help to overcome them.

2) Pray to God in the Name of His Son (Yeshua) and praise (thank) Him much.

3) Read God's Word (the Bible) once or more every day. Just as you have three square physical meals daily, you need regular spiritual meals. Before you read, pray for God to show you the truth as you read. He is the Author. It is *His* Book.

4) Memorize as many Bible verses as you can. (Start with the verses in this chapter.)

5) Fellowship at least weekly with other Bible believers.

After trying the best the world has to offer and now walking with the Messiah for more than 40 years, I can honestly say there is nothing that satisfies like knowing God in a personal, intimate way.

Commentary by Sid Roth

Many people say to me, "You have been a Jewish believer in Jesus for more than 30 years. Do you still believe in 'Him' as fervently as you did in the beginning? Don't you doubt the experience you had almost a quarter of a century ago? Don't you think you imagined it?"

If that were my only experience, I would have probably stopped following the Messiah many years ago. But my faith is based on two things: the *Spirit* of God and the *Word* of God.

First, the Spirit of God literally lives inside of me. As I am writing to you, I feel His presence. It's like rivers of living water flowing through my body. It's wonderful. I have never been high on drugs or drunk on alcohol, but I can't imagine any high that could come close to what I am experiencing now. I know God is with me all the time. I have seen sickness leave when I say His Name. I have spoken in a language I had never even *heard* previously, let alone learned, and led a man to know Jesus. I have what the Bible calls a peace that passes human understanding. So when someone asks me, "Don't you think you should forget about this Jesus stuff?" I respond, "It's too late. I've already experienced Him. I know Him!"

Second, my faith is based on the prophecies in the Jewish Scriptures. Most of God's predictions about His Jewish people have already come to pass. We can have full confidence that the remaining prophecies will come true as well.

The Scriptures tell about an event that will cause the prophetic time clock to accelerate. Jeremiah says there will be a large exodus of Jews from the land of the north (north of Israel is the former Soviet Union; see Jer. 16:15). Once this happens, the Jewish people in *all* the nations of the world will return. The prophet Ezekiel says not one will be left in the Diaspora (see Ezek. 39:28).

Isaiah says the Jews from China will return to Israel as a sign of the last days (see Isa. 49:12; *Sinim* is Hebrew for China). Most people have never heard of Chinese Jews. But I have been to Kaifeng, China, and met many Chinese Jews who are in the process of returning to Israel.

How will God cause an American Jew to return to Israel? After all, we would not only have to give up our American lifestyle, we would have to face the unique dangers of living in Israel as well.

Jeremiah 16:16 answers this question. First, there will be a season of mercy. "Fishermen" will gently tell the Jewish people that the floods are coming and the only ark of safety will be in the loving arms of Messiah.

But those who do not heed the warning will become victims of the "hunters." Past generations have seen these hunters: Pharaoh, Haman, Stalin, and Hitler. The only place a Jew will be able to find refuge from the new hunters will be in Israel.

Even so, the Bible says *all* nations will turn against Israel in the last days (see Zech. 14:2). Two-thirds of the Jewish people will perish (see Zech. 13:8).

When no hope is left, the Messiah will fight for Israel (see Zech. 14:3). The nation will repent (see Zech. 12:10) and be cleansed of sin (see Zech. 13:1).

You have two choices:

Either come to know the Messiah now and fulfill your destiny by becoming a champion for God, or believe in Him at the last great battle when He rescues us from destruction. The only problem with the latter choice is most of the Jewish people will perish before the great rescue. I believe most of the American Jews will not recognize the American, anti-Semitic deathtrap until it is too late. That was our fate in Hitler's Germany. And death without forgiveness of sin results in eternal separation from God, with no chance of reversal.

If you are not Jewish, your decision becomes even more critical. As you know, the first followers of Jesus were all Jewish! If you wanted to follow Jesus, the requirement was to convert to traditional Judaism. After Peter had a revelation from God, it was decided a Gentile could believe in Jesus without converting to Judaism. The flood gates were opened, and even more Gentiles than Jews followed the Jewish Messiah. But Jesus said in Luke 21:24 that when Jerusalem was in Jewish hands, it would signify the end of the Gentile age.

Jerusalem is in Jewish possession. *We are at the end of the Gentile age.* Multitudes of Gentiles will still be swept into His Kingdom, but those who resist will harden their hearts, and their love will grow cold. *Time is running short!* Some reading this book will be alive during the apocalyptic disasters predicted in the Bible. Others might die tonight. You don't know when your end will come. Now is the only moment you have for sure. Make it count.

After you have prayed to make the Messiah your Lord, or if you have any questions or want to locate a congregation in your area, write or fax me at the address or number on page 239.

Endnotes

1. See http://www.answers.com/topic/compound-probability.

2. Josephus, *Jewish Antiquities* (Cambridge, MA: Harvard UP, 1998).

3. Moses Maimonides, *The Thirteen Principles of Faith* (Brooklyn, NY: Kol Menachem, 2007).

Sid Roth's It's Supernatural! and Messianic Vision
P.O. Box 1918
Brunswick, GA 31521-1918

(912) 265-2500
(912) 265-3735 fax

Web Site: WW.Sidroth.org E-Mail: Info@Sidroth.org

Messianic Vision Canada
Suite 143
5929 L Jeanne D'arc Blvd. Orleans,
Ontario K1c 7k2

E-Mail: Canada@Sidroth.Org

Additional copies of this book and other book titles from DESTINY IMAGE are available at your local bookstore.

Call toll-free: 1-800-722-6774.

Send a request for a catalog to:

Destiny Image® Publishers, Inc.
P.O. Box 310
Shippensburg, PA 17257-0310

*"Speaking to the Purposes of God for This
Generation and for the Generations to Come."*

**For a complete list of our titles,
visit us at www.destinyimage.com.**